LET'S GO CAMPING!

12/4

Please renew or return items by the date
shown on your receipt

www.hertsdirect.org/libraries

Renewals and
enquiries: 0300 123 4049

Textphone for hearing
or speech impaired   0300 123 4041

Hertfordshire

LET'S GO CAMPING!

crochet your
own adventure

Kate Bruning

KYLE BOOKS

To my favourite campers, Jonno, Archie and Hugo. And of course, my Mum! This book is yours.

First published in Great Britain in 2015 by
Kyle Books, an imprint of Kyle Cathie Ltd
192–198 Vauxhall Bridge Road,
London SW1V 1DX
general.enquiries@kylebooks.com
www.kylebooks.com

Printer line 10 9 8 7 6 5 4 3 2 1

ISBN 978 0 85783 319 8

Designer: Mark Latter
Photographer: Keiko Oikawa
Illustrator: Kuo Kang Chen
Stylist: Christine Leech
Project Editor: Sophie Allen
Copy Editor: Katie Hardwicke
Pattern Editor: Joanne Scrace
Editorial Assistant: Hannah Coughlin
Production: Nic Jones, Gemma John and Lisa Pinnell

A Cataloguing in Publication record for this title is available from the British Library.

Colour reproduction by ALTA London
Printed and bound in Malaysia by Tien Wah Press

With kind permission of Geobra Brandstätter GmbH & Co. KG, Germany. PLAYMOBIL is a registered trademark of Geobra Brandstätter GmbH & Co. KG, for which also the displayed PLAYMOBIL toy figures are protected.

contents

Introduction   06

Crochet Techniques
and Abbreviations   08
Finishing Techniques   14
Materials   16
Patterns   18

Carefree Camping   18
Caravan Wishes   30
Ice Cream Supreme   44
Lakeside Memories   58
Canal Boat Idyll   82
Setting the Scene   98
Dressing Up   106

Index   110
Acknowledgements   112

introduction

When I was little, growing up in Australia, my day was spent knee deep in Lego, cardboard and sticky tape, lost in a miniature world of my own making. Then, when my two sons came along, I found that I had a wonderful excuse to revisit my childhood. Once again, my house was filled with the 'rip, rrrrrrip, rip' sound of sticky tape and the sharp grind of scissors. But, instead of the fairy houses and castles from my youth, our projects were wilder, crazier and much more dangerous.

You might ask what this has to do with a book on camping, or crochet? For me, crochet is a direct portal into my imagination and all of the boys' outward bound projects fed an idea that grew over time. How to incorporate those little tents, trees and boats that we had created from cardboard into a world of crochet. This seedling began to shoot away when we travelled around Europe and the UK. We stayed in all sorts of amazing places, including a renovated shepherd's hut, YHA cabins and even a castle. The boys spent hours talking about building their own hut back home in New Zealand, renovating a caravan and making a camping site on our farm's estuary. And I began to dream of my own version...

crochet techniques

how to begin

There are many ways to hold a crochet hook and yarn but I find this to be a quick and effective method. With your dominant hand, take the free end of the yarn and hold it in front of your other hand. Wrap the yarn once around the base of your little finger, then draw the yarn to the front, then up and over the index finger on the final joint. Bring the yarn back through to the palm side, between the index and middle fingers. Secure the yarn with the middle finger and thumb.

Keep your ring and little finger together. Raise the index finger to create a triangle of yarn.

Using your dominant hand, hold the crochet hook like a pencil with the hooked tip facing towards the yarn and the flattened middle section held between the thumb and pointer finger. Let the blunt end of the hook poke out of the space between the thumb and index finger. With the crochet hook facing up, bring it behind the length of yarn running from the index finger to the thumb and middle finger. *Push the yarn forward and bring the index and middle fingers together.

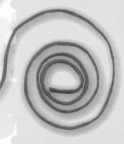

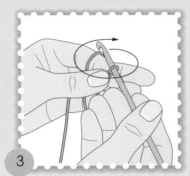

3 Rotate the hook 360 degrees so a little twist occurs in the yarn held between the index and middle fingers.** There should now be a loop around the crochet hook.

4 Replace the index finger with the middle finger to hold the twist and raise the index finger again. You are now ready to begin crocheting. Another way to begin is to create a slip knot and then follow the instructions of how to hold the yarn, leaving out the steps between * and **.

how to make a slip knot

Make a loop with the yarn and then bring the cut end of the yarn across the underside of the loop. It should now look like a cat's eye.

Draw the underside length of yarn up through the loop and then poke your crochet hook through the loop. Pull on the cut end of the yarn to adjust the loop until it is an appropriate size to begin crocheting with. Follow the directions in 'how to begin' until *.

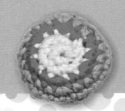

how to create a chain (ch)

With the hook pointing up and held in front of the yarn, swivel to wrap the yarn around the hook and then turn the hook forward, then downward to lock the yarn into place (I often refer to this action as grabbing the yarn). Draw the locked yarn through the loop on the crochet hook.

Repeat this action as many times as required to form the appropriate length of chain.

how to work a slip stitch (ss)

Insert the crochet hook through the stitch/chain as indicated by the diagram 1. Grab the yarn and pull it back through the stitch/chain. There should now be two loops on the crochet hook. Draw the first loop through the second loop.

how to work a double crochet (dc)

With the hook facing down, insert the crochet hook through the stitch/chain. Grab the yarn, then pull it back through the stitch/chain.

There should now be two loops on the crochet hook. Grab the yarn again and draw it through both loops.

how to work a half treble crochet (htr)

Wrap the yarn around the crochet hook once, then insert the crochet hook through the stitch/chain. Grab the yarn, pull it back through the stitch/chain.

There should now be three loops on the crochet hook. Grab the yarn and draw through all three loops.

how to work a treble crochet (tr)

With the hook facing down, wrap the yarn around the crochet hook, then insert the crochet hook through the stitch/chain. Grab the yarn then pull it back through the stitch/chain. There should now be three loops on the crochet hook. Grab the yarn and draw it through the first two loops. Grab the yarn again and draw it through the two loops left on the hook.

how to work a double treble crochet (dtr)

Wrap the yarn around the hook twice, then insert the hook through the stitch/chain. Grab the yarn then pull it back through the stitch/chain. There should now be four loops on the crochet hook. Grab the yarn and draw it through the first two loops. Grab the yarn and draw it through the next two loops on the hook. Grab the yarn again and pull it through the last two loops on the hook.

how to work a round

In this book, a round is worked in continuous spirals in the same direction. This is useful for making circles and three-dimensional projects. I always suggest using a slip stitch to finish off the first round as it makes for a neat finish.

how to work a row

Rows are worked from side to side and are turned at the end of every row. This is useful for making flat sections.

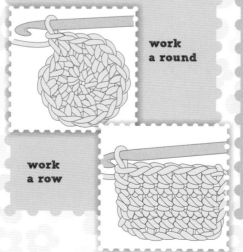

work a round

work a row

how to change from a row to a round in one pattern

It is important to note that many patterns in this book change between working in rounds and rows. Check at the beginning of each step to see whether it is worked in a row or round.

To switch from a row to a round is an easy process that usually calls in the preceding row to ch1 and turn. Work back along the previous row until reaching the corner stitch. The pattern will state whether you either work 1dc into it or (1dc, ch2, 1dc) back into the same st to create a flat corner.

I usually work into the side edges (row ends) for patterns crocheted in double crochet by working 1dc into every row ending.

N.B. I work into the foundation chain across the bottom of the piece rather than the first row worked into the foundation chain. If you don't do this, it may affect your final count of the round.

how to work a colour change

With the hook facing down, insert the crochet hook through the stitch/chain. Using the first colour, grab the yarn, then pull it back through the stitch/chain. There should now be two loops on the crochet hook.

Change to the new colour. Grab the new colour yarn and draw it through both loops.

how to fasten off

At the end of working your piece of crochet you need to fasten off to prevent the yarn from unravelling.

Remove the loop from the hook. Pull the loop a little to make it larger, but not so that it unravels.

Cut the yarn, leaving a tail of about 10cm, or longer if required, and then pass the cut end through the loop and pull tightly to close. The yarn end needs to be long enough to darn in when the project is finished.

how to read a pattern

For example: Row 24. 1dc, sk one st. 32dc, sk one st. 1dc into the last st. Ch1, turn. (34)

Row 24 – indicates whether it is worked from side to side (row) or in a continuous spiral (round) and also indicates how many rows/rounds will have been completed by the time the row is completed.
32dc – this means that 1dc is crocheted into each of the following 32 stitches.
Ch1 – this means to chain 1, which gives the appropriate height to the following row. For instance, a treble crochet row would begin with a chain 3 (ch3).
Turn – when a pattern is worked in rows (from one end to the other end), the crochet piece is flipped to the other side at the end of the row.
(34) – this is the stitch count and indicates the amount of stitches completed at the end of the row/round just worked. Stitch counts are not always included, as some patterns that involve stitches, such as a shell stitch, are easier to count in smaller increments. Brackets with instructions inside them: (1dc, ch2, 1dc) indicate that they all go into the same stitch unless otherwise directed.

tension

Because I am not recommending specific yarns, I do not give tension gauges for the projects. Instead, the projects will work just as well in a smaller ply, meaning that you can make the items as tiny or as enormous as you see fit – imagine a mouse-sized caravan made from 4ply!

However, in some of the projects an approximation of the final dimensions is given as a guide, although it will only apply if you are using the same ply yarn and hook.

abbreviations
BLO= back loop only
ch = chain
chsp = chain space
dc = double crochet
dtr = double treble crochet
FLO = front loop only
htr = half treble crochet
sk = skip
ss = slip stitch
cl = cluster
RS = right side
st/sts = stitch/stitches
tr = treble crochet

finishing techniques

washi tape bunting

Washi tape is a decorative masking tape originating from Japan and comes in a multitude of colours and patterns. In the Camping and Canal Boat scenes, I have used bunting made with washi tape for extra decoration. It is very simple to make and adds a nice contrast to the crochet projects.

Cut a length of cotton sewing thread (I used approximately 24cm for the tent bunting, and 16cm for the Canal Boat bunting) and lay it on the table.

Cut a 3cm length of washi tape and place it vertically beneath the thread, sticky side up.

Make sure that the thread is in the centre of the tape then fold the tape over.

Trim to a triangle or pennant shape.

bamboo skewers wrapped in washi tape

In some of the patterns, bamboo skewers covered in washi tape are used. It is a very simple and effective trick, particularly for projects such as the teepee.

Lay the bamboo skewer along the edge of a length of washi tape (sticky side up) and roll, smoothing the tape so that it sticks evenly. Then trim to the desired length.

embroidery stitches

Most of the embroidery requirements are very simple and only need variations of straight stitches. However, there are two decorative stitches that are essential:

French knots

French knots produce a textured stitch that is perfect for flower heads.

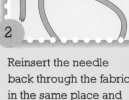

1

Bring the needle through to the front of the fabric. Hold the needle vertically and wrap the thread around once or twice, for a traditional French knot. Push the wraps down towards the fabric. Hold in place with your thumb.

2

Reinsert the needle back through the fabric in the same place and pull through to create a decorative knot.

3

In patterns such as the flowers or the pot plants, I recommend wrapping the needle 4-5 times for a larger knot.

4

daisy stitch A daisy stitch creates a curved line and is handy for embroidering ice creams and ice lollies onto the blackboard (see page 55).

1. Bring the needle through to the front of the fabric.

2. Without pulling tight, push the needle back through the fabric at the place your shape will end.

3. Gently press the loop left between the two points into the desired shape and then bring the needle back through to the top of the curve.

4. Secure the curve with a tiny stitch.

materials

yarns
I am loathe to make yarn recommendations. I love the thought of yarn as paint and making individual choices that suit your taste and of using what you have.

Occasionally a certain yarn may work well for a project such as DK cotton, which is very good for more structural patterns. When this is the case I make a 'yarn suggestion' but it is a suggestion only.

Many of the patterns only require a small amount of yarn. Where larger amounts of 50g or more are used, the number of balls of yarn required will be specified in the pattern.

crochet hooks

Because so many of these projects are structural and work well with a firm tension, I recommend smaller hooks than those that are usually matched with the yarn.

construction materials

If you peered into my toolbox for the projects in this book, you may be surprised by what lurks within. You will find:

- cardboard or artboard that is at least 500gsm or 1000 microns for reinforcing walls, floors, ceilings and so on
- bamboo skewers, which make wonderful poles
- washi tape for gussying up skewers and making bunting
- lots of lightweight cotton fabrics such as Liberty Lawn (my all time favourite) for wallpaper and sails
- little lengths of my grandmother's vintage lace are carefully stowed

and have become essential for curtain-making in projects such as the cabin and caravan

- high-loft wadding (or batting) and polyester stuffing for giving weight and substance to beds, boxes and so on
- a fine sewing needle and thread (I always use white because I'm lazy!) and embroidery needles
- buttons and beads for door knobs and decoration
- decorative paper drinking straws, which are very handy for bed-legs and sailboat masts
- a craft (Stanley) knife
- duct tape, which is the best way of attaching pieces of cardboard together.

It is all very useful, a little bit pretty and slightly subversive… just the way all good toolboxes should be.

glue

For a long time I was a purist and hand-stitched all of the details in my projects. And then I discovered glue! Often gluing a detail creates a better finish, as sewing on small details, such as a wheel onto a caravan, can sometimes warp the crochet. Of course, there are different glues for different jobs. Here are the two main glues that I use.

Ultra Thick PVA

I have just discovered this revolutionary glue! It is perfect for fabrics as it is so thick that it doesn't soak into the fibres. It also has enough stickiness that it will hold difficult to glue areas instantly but still allow for repositioning.

Hot Glue Gun

A hot glue gun is essential to some of the projects in the book as it is perfect for structural gluing – making bamboo skewer frames, for example – and sets almost instantly to give a strong bond.

Carefree Camping

We did a lot of camping when I was growing up in Australia. Looking back now from the relative safety of New Zealand, devoid of snakes and poisonous spiders (although it can be a little shaky on occasion), I am amazed that we survived. At the height of summer, we would unpack our tents, tables and chairs by a creek and make enough noise to hopefully scare away anything with fangs. Zips on tents had to be kept firmly closed at all times and if you had to walk somewhere, it was a good idea to bang a stick in front of you to send snakes slithering. It must have worked because I am here today, making a whimsical version of our camping holidays. No zips, snake scaring sticks or drab khaki canvas here.

Patterns in this Section

Tent
Sleeping bag
Sleeping mat
Teepee rug
Teepee
Picnic basket
Picnic rug
Campfire
Frying pan
Bunting

tent

for the tent

yellow DK yarn
3.5mm crochet hook
2 paper straws
4 bamboo skewers
washi tape
hot glue gun

Yarn suggestion: I have used cotton with a matte finish for a canvas-like effect.

Foundation row. Beginning from the top of the tent, using yellow yarn and a 3.5mm crochet hook, ch23.

Row 1. Starting in 2nd ch from hook, 21dc, 2dc into the last ch, 21dc along the opposite side of the foundation ch. Ch1, turn. (44)

Row 2 and all even rows. 1dc into every st. Ch1, turn.

Row 3. 2dc into the first st, 20dc, 2dc into each of the next 2 sts. 20dc. 2dc into the last st. Ch1, turn. (48)

Row 5. 1dc, 2dc into the next st, 20dc, 2dc into the next st, 2dc, 2dc into the next st, 20dc, 2dc into the next st, 1dc. Ch1, turn. (52)

Row 7. 2dc, 2dc into the next st, 20dc, 2dc into the next st, 4dc, 2dc into the next st, 20dc, 2dc into the next st, 2dc. Ch1, turn. (56)

Row 9. 3dc, 2dc into the next st, 20dc, 2dc into the next st, 6dc, 2dc into the next st, 20dc, 2dc into the next st, 3dc. Ch1, turn. (60)

Row 11. 4dc, 2dc into the next st, 20dc, 2dc into the next st, 8dc, 2dc into the next st, 20dc, 2dc into the next st, 4dc. Ch1, turn. (64)

Row 13. 5dc, 2dc into the next st, 20dc, 2dc into the next st, 10dc, 2dc into the next st, 20dc, 2dc into the next st, 5dc. Ch1, turn. (68)

Row 15. 6dc, 2dc into the next st, 20dc, 2dc into the next st, 12dc, 2dc into the next st, 20dc, 2dc into the next st, 6dc. Ch1, turn. (72)

Row 17. 7dc, 2dc into the next st, 20dc, 2dc into the next st, 14dc, 2dc into the next st, 20dc, 2dc into the next st, 7dc. Ch1, turn. (76)

Row 19. 8dc, 2dc into the next st, 20dc, 2dc into the next st, 16dc, 2dc into the next st, 20dc, 2dc into the next st, 8dc. Fasten off. (80)

to construct the frame

Cover the four bamboo skewers with washi tape (see page 14).

Measure the side of the crochet from point a. to c. (see diagram) then double this figure.

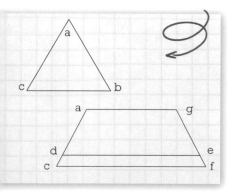

Cut two straws to this length and then fold in the middle.

Measure the length between c. and b. and then cut two pieces of skewer to this length.

Using a pin, make a hole in the bent straw at the same height just above points

c. and b. and facing towards each other.

Add a dab of hot glue then insert the skewer into the holes.

Repeat with the other straw for the other end of the tent.

Repeat these steps with points d. and e., to make the base, poking holes into the front side of the straws so that the two straws are joined to each other by two skewers.

Measure the length between the top of two straws (points a. and g.) once the base skewers have been inserted and cut a length of skewer to fit.

Make one more hole at the top of each straw.

Dab hot glue onto the holes and then insert the skewer.

Place the tent over the frame. Sew the corners of the tent to the corners of the straws and skewers.

sleeping bag + sleeping mat

for the sleeping bag

red 4ply yarn
3mm crochet hook

for the sleeping mat

turquoise 4ply yarn
2.5mm crochet hook
wadding

for the bag

Foundation row. Beginning at the bottom, using red yarn and a 3mm crochet hook, ch13.

Round 1. Starting in 2nd ch from hook, 11dc, 2dc into the last ch, 11dc along the opposite side of the foundation ch. (22)

Rounds 2–18. 1dc into every st. Fasten off.

hood

Row 1. Ch 2, 3dc into the second ch from hook. Ch1, turn. (3)

Row 2. 2dc into every st. Ch1, turn. (6)

Row 3. *1dc, 2dc into the next st. Repeat from * twice more. Ch1, turn. (9)

Row 4. *2dc, 2dc into the next st. Repeat from * twice more. Ch1, turn. (12)

Row 5. *3dc, 2dc into the next st. Repeat from * twice more. Ch1, turn. (15)

Row 6. *4dc, 2dc into the next st. Repeat from * twice more. Fasten off. (18)

Sew the hood to the back of the bag.

Work 1dc into every stitch around the front of the bag and around the hood.

Fasten off.

for the mat

Foundation row. Using turquoise yarn and a 2.5mm crochet hook, ch25.

Round 1. Starting in 2nd ch from hook, 23dc, 2dc into the last ch, 23dc along the opposite side of the foundation chain. (48)

Rounds 2–10. 1dc into every st. Fasten off.

Trace around the sleeping mat onto wadding and cut out.

Place the wadding inside the sleeping mat and then stitch up.

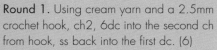

teepee rug

Round 1. Using cream yarn and a 2.5mm crochet hook, ch2, 6dc into the second ch from hook, ss back into the first dc. (6)

Round 2. 2dc into every st. (12)

Round 3. Change to yellow yarn. *1dc, 2dc into the next st. Repeat from * until the end of the round. (18)

Round 4. Change to cream yarn. *2dc, 2dc into the next st. Repeat from * until the end of the round. (24)

Round 5. *3dc, 2dc into the next st. Repeat from * until the end of the round. (30)

Round 6. Change to pink yarn. *4dc, 2dc into the next st. Repeat from * until the end of the round. (36)

Round 7. Change to cream yarn. *5dc, 2dc into the next st. Repeat from * until the end of the round. (42)

Round 8. *6dc, 2dc into the next st. Repeat from * until the end of the round. (48)

Round 9. Change to royal blue yarn. *7dc, 2dc into the next st. Repeat from * until the end of the round. (54)

Round 10. Change to cream yarn. *8dc, 2dc into the next st. Repeat from * until the end of the round. (60)

Round 11. *9dc, 2dc into the next st. Repeat from * until the end of the round. (66)

Round 12. Change to pale blue yarn. *10dc, 2dc into the next st. Repeat from * until the end of the round. (72)

Round 13. Change to cream yarn. *11dc, 2dc into the next st. Repeat from * until the end of the round. (78)

Round 14 .*12dc, 2dc into the next st. Repeat from* until the end of the round. (84)

Round 15. Change to red yarn. *13dc, 2dc into the next st. Repeat from * until the end of the round. (90)

Round 16. Change to cream yarn. *14dc, 2dc into the next st. Repeat from * until the end of the round. (96)

Round 17. *15dc, 2dc into the next st. Repeat from * until the end of the round. (102)

Round 18. Change to navy blue yarn. *16dc, 2dc into the next st. Repeat from * until the end of the round. Fasten off. (108)

teepee

for the teepee

turquoise DK yarn

cream DK yarn

3.5mm crochet hook

2.5mm crochet hook

assorted 4ply yarn
for embroidery

4 x bamboo skewers

washi tape

Foundation row. Beginning at the top of the teepee, using turquoise yarn and a 3.5mm crochet hook, ch7.

Row 1. Starting in 2nd ch from hook, 6dc. Ch1, turn. (6)

Row 2. *1dc, 2dc into the next st. Repeat from * twice more. Ch1, turn. (9)

Row 3. *2dc, 2dc into the next st. Repeat from * twice more. Ch1, turn. (12)

Row 4. 1dc into every st. Ch1, turn.

Row 5. *3dc, 2dc into the next st. Repeat from* twice more. Ch1, turn. (15)

Row 6. *4dc, 2dc into the next st. Repeat from* twice more. Ch1, turn. (18)

Row 7. As Row 4.

Row 8. *5dc, 2dc into the next st. Repeat from * twice more. Ch1, turn. (21)

Row 9. *6dc, 2dc into the next st. Repeat from * twice more. Ch1, turn. (24)

Row 10. As Row 4.

Row 11. *7dc, 2dc into the next st. Repeat from * twice more. Ch1, turn. (27)

Row 12. *8dc, 2dc into the next st. Repeat from * twice more. Ch1, turn. (30)

Row 13. As Row 4.

Row 14. *9dc, 2dc into the next st. Repeat from * twice more. Ch1, turn. (33)

Row 15. *10dc, 2dc into the next st. Repeat from * twice more. Ch1, turn. (36)

Row 16. As Row 4.

Row 17. *11dc, 2dc into the next st. Repeat from * twice more. Ch1, turn. (39)

Row 18. *12dc, 2dc into the next st. Repeat from * twice more. Ch1, turn. (42)

Row 19. As Row 4.

Row 20. *13dc, 2dc into the next st. Repeat from * twice more. Ch1, turn. (45)

Row 21. *14dc, 2dc into the next st. Repeat from * twice more. Ch1, turn. (48)

Row 22. As Row 4.

Row 23. *15dc, 2dc into the next st. Repeat from * twice more. Ch1, turn. (51)

Row 24. *16dc, 2dc into the next st. Repeat from * twice more. Ch1, turn. (54)

Row 25. As Row 4.

Row 26. *17dc, 2dc into the next st. Repeat from * twice more. Ch1, turn. (57)

Row 27. *18dc, 2dc into the next st. Repeat from * twice more. Fasten off. (60)

Round 28. Using cream yarn and a 3.5mm crochet hook, work 1dc into every st around the teepee and (1dc, ch1, 1dc) into every corner. Fasten off. (120)

for the embroidery

Using red yarn and a 2.5mm crochet hook, create a chain that runs the length of Row 22.

Sew the chain along Row 22.

Repeat this three more times for Rows 16, 10 and 4.

Embroider French knots in between the decorative chains (see page 15).

to construct the teepee

Sew the top of the teepee together from Row 1 to Row 8. Leave an opening at the top for the skewers to poke out.
Cover the bamboo skewers with washi tape (see page 14).

Making sure they are evenly spaced, sew the skewers inside the teepee to form poles. Cut the pointy ends off the skewers so that the 'poles' look in scale with the teepee.

picnic basket

picnig rug

for the picnic basket

yellow 4ply yarn
2.5mm crochet hook
red beads
glue

for the picnic rug

pale blue 4ply yarn
pale pink 4ply yarn
red 4ply yarn
cream 4ply yarn
2.5mm crochet hook

for the picnic basket

Foundation row. Using yellow yarn and a 2.5mm crochet hook, ch8.
Row 1. Starting in 2nd ch from hook, 7dc. Ch1, turn. (7)
Rows 2–5. 1dc into every st. Ch1, turn.

Rounds 6–9. 1dc into every st around each side. Fasten off. (24)
Ch11 for the handle.

Sew the handle onto the basket and fill with red beads for berries.

for the picnic rug

Round 1. Using pale blue yarn and a 2.5mm crochet hook, ch4 then ss back into the first ch.
Round 2. Working into the ch4 loop, ch3 (counts as 1tr), 2tr, ch3, *3tr, ch3. Repeat from * twice more, ss back into the top of the first ch3.
Round 3. Join pale pink yarn into any 3chsp, ch3 (counts as 1tr), 2tr, ch3, 3tr into the same chsp from the previous round, *3tr, ch3, 3tr into the next 3chsp. Repeat from * twice more, ss back into the top of the first ch3.
Round 4. Join red yarn into any 3chsp, ch3 (counts as 1tr), 2tr, ch3, 3tr all into the same chsp, 3tr in space between groups of trebles, *3tr, ch3, 3tr in next chsp, 3tr in space between groups of trebles. Repeat from *

twice more. Ss into top of ch3.
Round 5. Join cream yarn into any 3chsp, ch3 (counts as 1tr), 2tr, ch3, 3tr all into the same chsp, *3tr into each of the next two spaces between groups of trebles. 3tr, ch3, 3tr into the next 3chsp. Repeat from* twice more. 3tr into each of the next two spaces between groups of trebles, ss back into the top of the first ch3.
Round 6. Change to pale blue yarn. 6dc into every 3chsp corner, 3dc into every space between groups of trebles, ss back into the first dc.
Round 7. *Ch3, sk one st, ss into the next st. Repeat from* until the end of the round. Fasten off.

campfire

for the campfire

flecked brown 4ply yarn
red 4ply yarn
orange 4ply yarn
2.5mm crochet hook
bamboo skewer

for the kindling

Foundation row. Using brown yarn and a 2.5mm crochet hook, ch12.
Row 1. Starting in 3rd ch from hook, 10htr. (10)
Fasten off, leaving a long tail to sew with. Cut a length of bamboo skewer to match. Lay the bamboo skewer lengthways along the crochet.

Sew the sides together.

To create a natural look, make some pieces of kindling without the bamboo as it makes them more flexible.

Sew the pieces of kindling into a bundle.

for the flames

Make between three to five flames alternating between red and orange yarn.

Foundation row. Using red yarn and a 2.5mm crochet hook, ch4.

Row 1. Starting in 2nd ch from hook, 3dc. Fasten off, leaving a long tail.

Sew to the top of the kindling bundle. Bring the tails through so they look like little flames.

frying pan

bunting

for the frying pan

Round 1. Using black yarn and a 2.5mm crochet hook, ch2, 6dc into the second ch from hook, ss back into the first dc. (6)

Round 2. 2dc into every st. (12)

Round 3. Working into BLO, 1dc into every st.

Round 4. 1dc into every st. Ss back into the first dc. Do not fasten off.

for the handle

Row 5. Ch4 from the ss.

Row 6. Starting in 2nd ch from hook, 3dc. Ss back into the frying pan.

Sew the sides of the of the handle together. Fasten off.

for the bunting

Foundation row. Using a 4ply cotton and a 2.5mm crochet hook, ch6.

Row 1. Starting in 2nd ch from hook, 5dc. Ch1, turn. (5)

Row 2. 1dc, sk one st, 3dc. Ch1, turn. (4)

Row 3. 1dc, sk one st, 2dc. Ch1, turn. (3)

Row 4. 1dc, sk one st, 1dc. Ch1, turn. (2)

Row 5. Sk the first st. 1dc. Fasten off. (1)

Repeat to make the number of flags required. Join them together by working 1dc into every st along the top of each triangle.

caravan
wishes

Oh, to have a caravan! This is the wish that turned into a teensy, tiny dream come true. Last year I found myself pouring over books, magazines and, of course, the internet, enamoured by the thought of having my very own caravan. One that could be decorated with wallpaper and chandeliers, floral cushions, crocheted blankets and pastel teacups. One that we could take our two energetic boys on holiday in… Which is where the dream began to sputter. And so, I made my own miniature version. If only I had some of Alice in Wonderland's 'drink me' potion…

Patterns in this Section

Caravan
Bunk beds
Bench
Cushions
Pillows
Blankets
Kitchen sink and cupboards
Cups

caravan

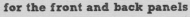

for the caravan

3 x 50g balls of cream DK yarn

3 x 50g balls of green DK yarn

silver 4ply yarn

pale blue 4ply yarn

black 4ply yarn

3.5mm crochet hook

2.5mm crochet hook

cardboard

lightweight cotton fabric, approx. 44 x 17cm

glue

1 button

1 red bead

duct tape

a small amount of lace for curtains

yarn suggestion: mercerised cotton is a good choice for the caravan as it provides a smooth texture and nice sheen

for the front and back panels
Make 2

Foundation row. Beginning at the bottom, using cream yarn and a 3.5mm hook, ch31.

Row 1. Starting in 2nd ch from hook, 30dc. Ch1, turn. (30)

Rows 2–3. 1dc, 2dc into the next st, dc across to the last 2sts, 2dc into the next st, 1dc. Ch1, turn.

Row 4. 1dc into every st. Ch1, turn. (34)

Row 5. As Row 2. (36)

Rows 6–7. 1dc into every st. Ch1, turn.

Row 8. As Row 2. (38)

Rows 9–10. 1dc into every st.

Rows 11–21. Change to green yarn. 1dc into every st. Ch1, turn.

Row 22. 1dc, sk one st, 34dc, sk one st, 1dc. Ch1, turn. (36)

Row 23. 1dc into every st. Ch1, turn.

Rows 24–31. 1dc, sk one st, dc to last 2sts, sk one st, 1dc. Ch1, turn. (20)

Row 32. 1dc, sk one st, dc to last 2sts, sk one st, 1dc. Ch1, turn. Fasten off. (18)

to construct the front panel: stage 1

Trace around the front panel onto cardboard and cut out a template. Make two more: one template is for the front panel (template A) and two are for the back panel (templates B and C).

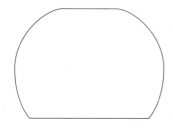

Take template A and cut out a matching piece of fabric with a 1cm margin on all sides. Glue the fabric to the cardboard. Cut notches around the margin then fold and glue the margin to the back of the cardboard template. Return to crocheting the front panel.

Round 1. With RS facing, using 3.5mm hook, attach green yarn to the row end at the start of the green section (Row 12). Work 61dc around the panel until reaching the beginning of Row 12. Fasten off. Change to cream yarn and work another 50dc, ss back into the first dc. Fasten off. (111)

Round 2. Reattach green yarn, *2dc, sk one st. Repeat from * 7 more times, 16dc, sk one st, *2dc sk one st. Repeat

from * 7 more times. Change to cream yarn. *2dc, sk one next st. Repeat from * two more times. 27dc, sk one st, *2dc, sk one st. Repeat from* two more times. 1dc, ss back into the first dc. Fasten off. (87)

Insert cardboard template A, fabric facing outwards, into the front panel then carefully glue the overlapping crochet border (formed by Round 2) to the front side of the fabric-covered cardboard template.

for the external panel (outer walls, floor and roof)

The panel is formed by crocheting around the edge of the back panel and is worked in two parts (a and b), one section for each colour (green and cream).

Row 1a. With RS facing, using a 3.5mm hook, attach green yarn to the row end at the start of the green section (Row 12). Work 61dc around the panel until reaching the beginning of Row 12. Ch1, turn. (61)

Rows 2a–21a. 1dc into every st. Ch1, turn. (61)

Row 22a. 1dc into every st. Fasten off. (61)

Row 1b. With RS facing, attach cream yarn to the row at the start of the cream section (Row 10). Work 50dc around the panel until reaching the end of Row 10. Ch1, turn. (50)

Rows 2b–21b. 1dc into every st. Ch1, turn. (50)

Row 22b. 1dc into every st. Fasten off. (50)

Sew the ends of the two panels together on both sides to make one continuous band that runs the entire length around the back panel.

to construct the cardboard caravan body

Measure the straight side of cardboard template C (the base), then the width of the crocheted external side panel (the outside walls). Cut a piece of cardboard to match. This will form the floor of the caravan (template D).

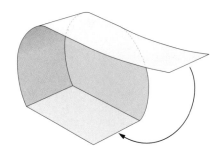

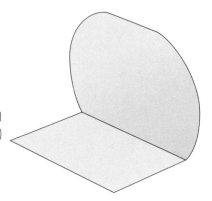

Measure the perimeter of template C from the right-hand side of the base, around the curve (the walls and the ceiling) to the left-hand side of the base. Cut a rectangle of cardboard to this length plus the width of template D, to make template E.

Gently bend template E to encourage a curve (see the illustration above).

Using duct tape, attach template D to the bottom of template C.

Tape template E around the curved sides of template C. Make little cuts into the tape so that it sticks to the curve neatly.

Tape the edges of templates D and E together.

Insert the cardboard caravan body into the crocheted caravan body.

to construct the wallpapered internal back wall

Take cardboard template B and reduce its size by cutting away a 3mm border around the template. Cut out a matching piece of fabric with a 1cm margin on all sides. Glue the fabric to the cardboard. Cut notches around the margin then fold and glue the margin to the back of the cardboard template.

for the internal panel (inner walls, floor and ceiling)

Foundation round. Using cream yarn and a 3.5mm hook, ch108 then ss back into the first ch.
Rounds 1–20. 1dc into every st. (108)
Round 21. *5dc, sk one st. Repeat from * until the end of the round. Fasten off. (90)

Insert the internal crochet side panel into the cardboard caravan body and stitch the internal and external panels around the edges.

Add some glue to the back wall (of the cardboard body) then push the fabric-covered cardboard panel against the back wall. This will secure the crocheted internal walls into place.

for the pin striping

Note: Pinstriping is the decorative silver stripe which runs around the outside of the caravan.

For the external front panel, using silver yarn and a 2.5mm crochet hook, create a length of chain that can run along the length of the front panel between Rows 10–11 (where the colour change occurs). Sew into place.

Repeat for the other side of the caravan.

for the button loop

Foundation row. Using green yarn and a 3.5mm hook, ch5.
Row 1. Starting in 2nd ch from hook, 4dc. Ch1, turn. (4)
Rows 2–5. 1dc into every st. Ch1, turn. (4)
Row 6. 1dc, sk the following 2sts, 1dc. Fasten off.

Sew to the top of the external front panel. Sew a button onto the caravan roof.

for the caravan door

Foundation row. Using cream yarn and a 3.5mm hook, ch12.
Row 1. Starting in 2nd ch from hook, 11dc. Ch1, turn. (11)
Rows 2–21. 1dc into every st. Ch1, turn.
Row 22. 1dc into every st. Fasten off.
Round 23. Using green yarn and a 3.5mm hook, work 21dc up one side of the door, (1dc, ch2, 1dc) into the corner st, 8dc, (1dc, ch2, 1dc) into the corner st, 21dc. Fasten off.

Using silver yarn and a 2.5mm hook, make a chain that is long enough to be sewn into the line between the cream and green crochet.

Sew on a red bead for a door handle. Glue the door in place on the front of the caravan.

for the windows

Make 2

Foundation row. Using pale blue yarn and a 2.5mm hook, ch19.

Row 1. Starting in 2nd ch from hook, 18dc. Ch1, turn. (18)

Rows 2–11. 1dc into every st. Ch1, turn.

Row 12. 1dc into every st. Fasten off.

Round 13. Using silver yarn and a 2.5mm hook, 1dc into every st around each side and (1dc, ch2, 1dc) into every corner. Fasten off. (62)

Cut a piece of lace to size and then sew to the internal window for a curtain.

Glue the windows into place as shown in the photographs, one internal and one external and line them up so they create the illusion of being the same window.

for the wheels

Make 3

for the tyre

Round 1. Using black yarn and a 2.5mm hook, ch2, 6dc into the 2nd ch from hook. (6)

Round 2. 2dc into every st. (12)

Round 3. *1dc, 2dc into the next st. Repeat from * until the end of the round. (18)

Round 4. *2dc, 2dc into the next st. Repeat from * until the end of the round. (24)

Round 5. *3dc, 2dc into the next st. Repeat from * until the end of the round. (30)

Round 6. *4dc, sk the next st. Repeat from * until the end of the round. (24)

Round 7. *3dc, sk the next st. Repeat from * until the end of the round. (18)

Round 8. *2dc, sk the next st. Repeat from * until the end of the round. (12)

Round 9. *1dc, sk the next st. Repeat from * until the end of the round. Fasten off. (6)

for the hubcap

Round 1. Using silver yarn and a 2.5mm hook, ch2, 6dc into the 2nd ch from hook. (6)

Round 2. 2dc into every st. (12)

Sew to the centre of the wheel and then glue into place, one on each side and the spare wheel underneath the back external window.

bunk beds

for the bunk beds
Make 2
Foundation row. Using teal yarn and a 2.5mm hook, ch 25.
Round 1. Starting in 2nd ch from hook, 23dc, 2dc into the last ch. Work 23dc along the opposite side of the chain. (48)
Rounds 2–12. 1dc into every st.
Fasten off leaving a long tail.

to construct the bunk
Trace around the bunk bed onto a piece of cardboard and cut out. Repeat with wadding.

Place the wadding and cardboard inside the bunk bed and then sew up the end.

Glue the bunks into place then carefully hammer dressmaking pins through the caravan and into the cardboard section of the bed.

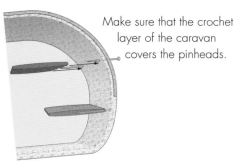

Make sure that the crochet layer of the caravan covers the pinheads.

Using a strong needle, thread with the cord for the bunk strings. Make a knot in the caravan ceiling just above the bunk and then thread down through the front corners of both bunk beds. Run the thread along the side of the bottom bunk and then back up through both bunks' far corners. Push the needle through the roof and then back down through the ceiling. Tie off.

for the bench
Repeat as for the bunk up until Round 8. Fasten off leaving a long tail.

to construct the bench
Repeat the first three steps for the bunk bed instructions above.

cushions

pillows

for the cushions

cream 4ply yarn
pink 4ply yarn
red 4ply yarn
royal blue 4ply yarn
pale blue 4ply yarn
2.5mm crochet hook
stuffing

for the pillow

cream 4ply yarn
2.5mm crochet hook
stuffing

for the round cushion

Round 1. Using cream yarn, ch2, 6dc into the 2nd ch from hook. (6)
Round 2. 2dc into every st. (12)
Round 3. Change to red yarn. *1dc, 2dc into the next st. Repeat from * until the end of the round. (18)
Round 4. Change to pink yarn. *2dc, 2dc into the next st. Repeat from * until the end of the round. (24)
Round 5. 1dc into every st.
Round 6. *3dc, sk one st. Repeat from * until the end of the round. (18)
Stuff.
Round 7. *2dc, sk one st. Repeat from * until the end of the round. (12)
Round 8. *1dc, sk one st. Repeat from * until the end of the round. (6)
Fasten off.

for the square cushion

Make one in pale blue and the other in royal blue.
Foundation row. Ch14, ss back into the first st.
Round 1. Ch1, 1dc into every st. (14)
Rounds 2–7. 1dc into every st.

Fasten off and then sew up one end with the tail.

Stuff and then sew up the other end.

for the pillow

Make 2
Foundation row. Ch14, ss back into the first st.
Round 1. Ch1, 1dc into every st. (14)
Rounds 2–10. 1dc into every st.

Close the end and then sew up.

Stuff and then sew up the other end.

blankets

for the blankets

yellow 4ply yarn
pale blue 4ply yarn
cream 4ply yarn
red 4ply yarn
pink 4ply yarn
2.5mm crochet hook

special stitches:

2trcl. *With the hook facing down, wrap the yarn around the hook then insert the crochet hook through the stitch/chain. Grab the yarn again then pull it back through the stitch/chain. Wrap the yarn around the hook again and draw it through the first two loops. Repeat from * one more time into the same st. There should now be 3 loops on the hook. Grab the yarn and pull it through all 3 loops.

3trcl. *With the hook facing down, wrap the yarn around the hook then insert the crochet hook through the stitch/chain. Grab the yarn again then pull it back through the stitch/chain. Wrap the yarn around the hook again and draw it through the first two loops. Repeat from * two more times into the same st. There should now be 4 loops on the hook. Grab the yarn and pull it through all 4 loops.

for the blankets

blanket 1

Round 1. Using yellow yarn, ch6, ss back into the first st.

Round 2. Working into the ch6 loop, ch2, 2trcl, ch3, *3trcl, ch3. Repeat from * two more times. Ss back into the ch2.

Round 3. Change to pale blue yarn. Into the first 3chsp, ch2, 2trcl, ch1. *Working into the next 3chsp, 3trcl, ch3, 3trcl, ch1. Repeat from * two more times. 3trcl into the last 3chsp, ch3, ss back into the ch2.

Round 4. Change to cream yarn. Into the first 3chsp, ch2, 2trcl, ch1. *Working into the next next 3chsp, 3trcl, ch3, 3trcl, ch1, 3trcl into the following 3chsp, ch1. Repeat from * two more times. 3trcl into the last 3chsp, ch3, ss back into the ch2.

Round 5. 3dc into each 1chsp, (3dc, ch2, 3dc) into every 3chsp (corner gap), ss back into the first dc. (48)

Round 6. Change to red yarn. Ch1, 1dc into every st, (1dc, ch2, 1dc) into each corner gap, ss back into the first dc. (52)

Round 7. Change to pink yarn. As Round 6. (56)

Fasten off.

blanket 2

Make nine squares from assorted colours of 4ply yarn.

Round 1. Using chosen colour yarn and a 2.5mm hook, ch4, ss back into the first ch.

Round 2. Working into the ch-4 loop, ch1, *3dc, ch2. Repeat from* three more times. Ss back into the first dc.

Round 3. Ch1, 1dc into every st and (1dc, ch2, 1dc) into each 2chsp, ss back into the first dc.

Sew the nine squares together.

for the edging

Round 1. Using pale blue, work 1dc in into every st around the blanket, ss back into the first dc.

Round 2. This step is for one side only. Sk the first st, *3tr into the next st. Sk one st, ss into the following st, sk one st. Repeat from * two more times. 3tr, sk one st, ss into the last st.

kitchen sink and cupboard

for the kitchen sink and cupboard

silver 4ply yarn
pink 4ply yarn
yellow 4ply yarn
2.5mm crochet hook
cardboard
duct tape
4 x blue beads
2 x metal beads
earring hook
hot glue gun

Note: the sink unit is worked in one piece, starting with the sink basin, then working the draining board and then the base.

Foundation row. Beginning at the bottom of the sink basin, using silver yarn and a a 2.5mm hook, ch8.

Row 1. Starting in 2nd ch from hook, 7dc. Ch1, turn. (7)

Rows 2–6. 1dc into every st to form the sides of the sink basin. Ch1, turn. (7)

Round 7. 1dc into every st around each side. (24)

Rounds 8–11. 1dc into every st.

Row 12. To create the draining board, working into FLO, 7dc. Ch1, turn.

Rows 13–23. 1dc into every st. Ch1, turn.

Round 24. 6dc, (1dc, ch2, 1dc) into the corner st, 11dc along the row ends of Rows 13–23 (the draining board). Working into BLO around the sink insert, 5dc, (1dc, ch2, 1dc) into the corner st, 5dc, (1dc, ch2, 1dc) into the corner st, 5dc. Resume working through both loops, 11dc along the opposite row ends of Rows 13–23, ch2, ss back into the first dc. (54)

Round 25. Working into BLO, 1dc into every st.

Round 26. 1dc into every st.

Rounds 27–38. Change to pink yarn. 1dc into every st.

Round 39. 1dc into every st. Ch1, turn.

Row 40. 9dc. Ch1, turn. (9)

Rows 41–54. 1dc into every st. Ch1, turn.

Row 55. 1dc into every st. Fasten off.

to construct the kitchen sink and cupboard

Measure the width and length of the base. Cut out a piece of cardboard to these measurements.

Repeat this step with all of the sides. Measure the cupboard top (exclude the sink insert) and cut a piece of cardboard to these measurements.

Tape all of the pieces together to create a rectangular cube with a gap for the sink to go into.

Insert the cardboard cube into the crochet cupboard and push the sink down through the gap.

Sew up the base.

for the larger cupboard door

Foundation row. Using yellow yarn and a 2.5mm crochet hook, ch8.

Row 1. Starting in 2nd ch from hook, 7dc. Ch1, turn. (7)

Rows 2–5. 1dc into every st. Ch1, turn.

Round 6. 1dc into every st around each side, (1dc, ch2, 1dc) into every corner st. (26)

Round 7. Change to silver yarn. 1dc into every st around the sides (1dc, ch2, 1dc) into every corner st. Fasten off. (32)

for the faucet and taps

Sew the earring hook onto the far side of the sink. Secure it with a dab of hot glue. Sew the metal beads onto either side of the faucet to become taps.

for the drawers

Make 2

Foundation row. Using yellow yarn and a 2.5mm crochet hook, ch6.

Row 1. Starting in 2nd ch from hook, 5dc. Ch1, turn. (5)

Row 2. 1dc into every st. Ch1, turn.

Round 3. Change to silver yarn. 1dc into every st around the sides (1dc, ch2, 1dc) into every corner st. Fasten off. (14)

to construct the larger cupboard door

I have a nifty trick to give the doors some body:

Cut a piece of duct tape and fold it back on itself, sticky side out.

Stick to the back of the doors then cut the tape so it doesn't show.

Stick the doors onto the front of the kitchen sink and then sew around the doors.

Sew beads on for door knobs.

for the long kitchen cupboard

Foundation row. Using pink yarn and a 2.5mm crochet hook, ch18.

Row 1. Starting in 2nd ch from hook, 17dc. Ch1, turn. (17)

Rows 2–8. 1dc into every st. Ch1, turn.

Round 9. 1dc into every st around each side. (48)

Rounds 10–13. 1dc into every st.

Round 14. Working into BLO, 1dc into every st.

Rounds 15–19. 1dc into every st.

Row 20. 17dc. Ch1, turn. (17)

Rows 21–26. 1dc into every st. Ch1, turn.

Row 27. 1dc into every st. Fasten off.

To construct the cupboard, see the method for the chest freezer on page 56.

for the door

Make 2

Foundation row. Using yellow yarn and a 2.5mm crochet hook, ch16.

Row 1. Starting in 2nd ch from hook 15dc. Ch1, turn. (15)

Rows 2–5. 1dc into every st. Ch1, turn.

Row 6. 1dc into every st. Fasten off.

to construct the long kitchen cupboard door

Measure the length and width of the cupboard door and cut a piece of cardboard to match.

Crochet the two cupboard doors together with the cardboard sandwiched inside as follows: Using silver yarn, 1dc into every st around the sides and (1dc, ch2, 1dc) into every corner st. Fasten off.

Sew one edge of the cupboard door to the cupboard.

Sew on a bead for the door knob.

for the cups

cream 4ply yarn

blue 4ply yarn

green 4ply yarn

2.5mm crochet hook

yarn suggestion: I use 4ply cotton thread as it gives excellent stitch definition to small projects.

Round 1. Using cream yarn, ch 2, 6dc into the 2nd ch from hook, ss back into the first dc.

Round 2. *Working into BLO, 1dc into the first st then 2dc into the next st*. Repeat from * two more times. (9)

Rounds 3–4. 1dc into every st. (9)

Round 5. Ss into every st. Do not fasten off.

To form the handle, ch3 then fasten off. Sew the end to the bottom of the cup.

Sew three cups in various colours to the underside of the long kitchen cupboard.

ice cream
supreme

Growing up, all hot days in summer were good. But the summer days, when the piped music of an ice cream van echoed through the streets, were golden. My legs would tense up like coiled springs and I would begin a frenzied dash around the house, simultaneously begging my mother for money whilst diving down the back of the couch for change. I'm afraid the response is still there. I recently found myself on holiday, running out onto the street in my nightie, whooping it up as the ice cream van swept by. Of course, any purchases were for my boys...

Patterns in this Section

Ice cream van
Windows
Headlights/grill and wheels
Rooftop ice cream
Appliqué ice creams
and ice lollies
Teensy tiny ice lollies
Chest freezer

ice cream van

for the ice cream van

2 × 50g balls of pink DK yarn

2 × 50g balls of cream DK yarn

1 × 50g ball of pale blue DK yarn

3.5mm crochet hook

cardboard

duct tape

craft knife

small button

stuffing

for the front panel

Foundation row. Beginning from the bottom of the panel and using pink yarn and a 3.5mm crochet hook, ch23.

Row 1. Starting in 2nd ch from hook, 22dc. Ch1, turn. (22)

Row 2. 1dc, 2dc into the next st, 20dc. Ch1, turn. (23)

Rows 3–5. 1dc into every st. Ch1, turn.

Row 6. 1dc, 2dc into the next st, 21dc. Ch1, turn. (24)

Rows 7–11. 1dc into every st. Ch1, turn.

This part is now worked in two sections (a and b) to form a gap for the concession window.

Rows 12a–16a. Change to cream yarn. 7dc. Ch1, turn. (7)

Row 17a. 5dc, sk one st, 1dc. Ch1, turn. (6)

Row 18a. 1dc into every st.

Fasten off.

Return to Row 12.

Rows 12b–15b. Working into Row 11, reattach the yarn leaving a 10 st gap for the window, then work as for the first side.

Row 16b. 1dc into every st. Ch9, turn.

Row 17b. Starting in the 2nd ch from hook, 15dc. Ch1, turn. (15)

Row 18b. 1dc into every st. Ch1, turn.

Row 19. 15dc, ch10, 6dc (across section a). Ch1, turn. (21)

Row 20. 1dc, sk one st, 4dc, 1dc into each ch, 13dc, sk one st, 1dc. Ch1, turn. (29)

Row 21. 1dc, sk one st, 27dc. Ch1, turn. (28)

Row 22. 1dc into every st. Ch1, turn.

Row 23. 1dc, sk one st, 24dc, sk one st, 1dc. Ch1, turn. (26)

Row 24. 1dc into every st. Ch1, turn.

Row 25. 1dc, sk one st, 22dc, sk one st, 1dc. Ch1, turn. (24)

Row 26. 1dc into every st. Fasten off.

for the back panel

Make 2

Repeat the instructions for the front panel until the end of Row 11 then work as follows:

Rows 12–15. Change to cream yarn. 1dc into every st. Ch1, turn. (24)

Row 16. 1dc into every st. Ch9, turn.

Row 17. Starting in the 2nd ch from hook, 8dc across the ch, 22dc, sk one st. 1dc into the last st. (31)

Rows 18–19. 1dc into every st. Ch1, turn. (31)

Row 20. 1dc, sk one st. 27dc, sk one st. 1dc. Ch1, turn. (29)

Rows 21–26. Work as for the front panel.

for the internal side panel (floor and back)

This section is worked in pale blue and cream stripes. Alternate the two colours, working two rows of each.

Foundation row. Beginning with cream yarn, ch49.

Row 1. Starting in the 2nd ch from hook, 48dc. Ch1, turn. (48)

Rows 2–17. 1dc into every st. Ch1, turn.

Row 18. 1dc into every st. Fasten off.

for the roof

Make 2

Make the external roof in cream yarn and the internal roof in cream and pale blue stripes, alternating colours every 2 rows.

Foundation row. Beginning with cream yarn, ch37.

Row 1. Starting in the 2nd ch from hook, 36dc. Ch1, turn. (36)

Rows 2–17. 1dc into every st. Ch1, turn.

Row 18. 1dc into every st. Fasten off.

to construct the cardboard body

Trace around the back panel onto cardboard and cut out two templates (templates 1 and 2).

Measure the length and width of the external side panel. Cut out a piece of cardboard to match. Cut into two pieces, one the length of the van base and the other the length of the curved side.

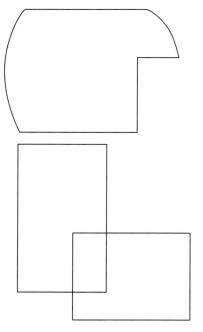

Using duct tape, tape the two pieces of cardboard to the bottom and curved side of the cardboard back panel.

Reinforce all of the joins with duct tape.

to construct the van body

Sew the external side panel around the bottom and side of the front panel. Repeat with the back panel.

Repeat this process with the internal set. Make sure the concession windows line up. Sandwich the cardboard van body with the internal and external layers of the crocheted van body. Sew around all of the edges.

Using a craft knife, cut out a cardboard rectangle where the concession windows line up. Take care not to cut any stitches. Sew the edges of the window together.

to construct the cardboard roof

Measure the length and width of the roof panel and cut out a piece of cardboard to match.

Measure the length of the van's roof and mark this on the cardboard. Cut along this line. The smaller piece will be template 3 and the longer piece, template 4.

Sew the internal and external roof panels together with both pieces of cardboard inside.

Sew the roof panel between the two pieces of cardboard sandwiched inside.

The panel will now be able to bend so that the roof can open.

Sew the end containing template 4 to the overhanging front of the van body.

for the button loop
Foundation row. Using cream yarn, ch5.
Row 1. Starting form the 2nd ch from hook, 4. Ch1, turn. (4)
Rows 2–4. 1dc into every st. Ch1, turn. (4)
Row 5. 1dc into every st. Ch5, turn and ss into the last st of the row.

Attach to the opening end of the roof panel.

for the concession window shutter
Make 2
Foundation row. Using cream yarn, ch12.
Row 1. Starting form the 2nd ch from hook, 11dc, turn. (11)
Rows 2–5. 1dc into every st. Ch1, turn. (11)
Row 6. 1dc into every st. Fasten off. (11)
Measure the shutter and cut out a piece of cardboard to match.

Sandwich the cardboard between the two shutters and sew together.

Sew one edge to the base of the window Using cream yarn, ch13. Sew this to the front edge of the shutter for a button loop.

Sew a button on the inside of the ice cream van above the concession window.

for the cab
The engine and cab are made from two separate parts. The first part makes up the windscreen section.

windscreen section
Foundation row. Using pink yarn, ch17.
Row 1. Starting in the 2nd ch from hook, 16dc. Ch1, turn. (16)
Rows 2–7. 1dc into every st. Ch1, turn.
Row 8. 1dc into every st. Fasten off.

for the hood and grill section
Foundation row. Using pink yarn, ch9.
Row 1. Starting form the 2nd ch from hook, 8dc. Ch1, turn. (8)
Rows 2–16. 1dc into every st. Ch1, turn.
Round 17. 7dc, 2dc into the corner st, 15dc along the front, 2dc into the corner st, 22dc. (48).
Ss back into the first dc.
Rounds 18–22. 1dc into every st.
Count 8 sts along from the last dc worked, line up the windscreen section with the front side of the hood. Sew these two sections together. Because the windscreen is 16dc long, make sure that when you are sewing the two sections together you only sew into 16dc on the hood.

Round 23. 8dc, pick up 8dc along the bonnet's side, 16dc along the bonnet's front, 8dc down the bonnet's side. 1dc into every st until the end of the round. (64)
Rounds 24–27. 1dc into every st. (52)
Round 28. 1dc into every st. Ch1, turn.
This section forms the back flap.
Row 29. 16dc. Ch1, turn. (16)
Rows 30–44 1dc into every st. Ch1, turn.
Row 45. 1dc into every st. Fasten off.

Measure the cab base and cut out a piece of cardboard to match.

Insert cardboard and stuff. Sew up the sides.

Sew the cab to the van.

windows

for the windows

pale blue 4ply yarn
silver 4ply yarn
2.5mm crochet hook
glue

for the side window
Make 2
Foundation row. Beginning from the bottom of the window, using pale blue yarn, ch7.
Row 1. Starting from the 2nd ch from the hook, 6dc. Ch1, turn. (6)
Row 2. 4dc, sk one st, 1dc. Ch1, turn. (5)
Row 3. 1dc into every st. Ch1, turn.
Row 4. 3dc, sk one st, 1dc. Fasten off. (4)
Round 5. Change to silver yarn. 1dc into every st, (1dc, ch1, 1dc) into every corner. Fasten off. (20)

Glue to the sides of the cab as shown in the photograph, with Row 4 at the top.

for the front windscreen
Foundation row. Using pale blue yarn, ch19.
Row 1. Starting from the 2nd ch from the hook, 18dc. Ch1, turn. (18)
Rows 2–5. 1dc into every st. Ch1, turn. (18)
Row 6. 1dc into every st.
Fasten off.

Change to silver yarn and work 1dc into every st and (1dc, ch1, 1dc) into every corner. Fasten off. (48)

Glue to the windscreen section of the cab.

**for the headlights
and grill and wheels**

yellow 4ply yarn
silver 4ply yarn
black 4ply yarn
2.5mm crochet hook

for the headlights and grill
Round 1. Using yellow yarn and a 2.5mm crochet hook, ch2, 6dc into the 2nd ch from hook, ss back into the first st. (6)

Glue or sew into place on either side of the bonnet.

Sew 4 lines of straight stitches with silver yarn between the headlights to create a grill.

for the tyres
Make 4
Round 1. Using black yarn, ch2, 6dc into the 2nd ch from hook, ss back into the first dc. (6)
Round 2. 2dc into every st. (12)

Round 3. *1dc, 2dc into the next st. Repeat from * until the end of the round. (18)
Round 4. *2dc, 2dc into the next st. Repeat from * until the end of the round. (24)
Round 5. *3dc, sk one st. Repeat from * until the end of the round. (18)
Round 6. *2dc, sk one st. Repeat from * until the end of the round. (12)
Round 7. *1dc, sk one st. Repeat from * until the end of the round. Fasten off. (6)

hubcaps
Make 4
Round 1. Using silver yarn, ch2, 6dc into the 2nd ch from hook, ss back into the first dc. (6)
Round 2. 2dc into every st. (12)

Sew to the centre of the tyre and glue or stitch the wheels into place.

for the rooftop ice cream

beige DK yarn
blue DK yarn
3.5mm crochet hook
stuffing

for the cone

Round 1. Beginning from the base of the cone, using beige yarn and a 3.5mm crochet hook, ch2, 4dc into the 2nd ch from hook, ss back into the first dc. (4)

Round 2. *1dc, 2dc into the next st. Repeat from * once more. (6)

Round 3. *2dc, 2dc into the next st. Repeat from * once more. (8)

Round 4. *3dc, 2dc into the next st. Repeat from * once more. (10)

Round 5. *4dc, 2dc into the next st. Repeat from * once more. (12)

Round 6. *5dc, 2dc into the next st. Repeat from * once more. (14)

Round 7. *6dc, 2dc into the next st. Repeat from * once more. (16)

Round 8. Working into FLO, *7htr, 2htr into the next st. Repeat from * once more. Fasten off. (18).

for the ice cream

Foundation row. Using blue yarn, ch68.

Row 1. Starting from the 3rd ch from hook, 66htr. (66)

Sew the chain to the top of the cone, coil the chain up to a peak, stitching as you go. Stuff the ice cream before the peak becomes too narrow. Sew to the roof of the truck.

for the appliqué ice creams and lollies

beige 4ply yarn	black 4ply yarn
pink 4ply yarn	2.5mm crochet hook
yellow 4ply yarn	
pale pink 4ply yarn	yarn needle
	red beads
pale blue 4ply yarn	1 red button

for the cone

Foundation row. Using beige yarn and a 2.5mm crochet hook, ch8.

Row 1. Starting from the 2nd ch from hook, 7dc. Ch1, turn. (7)

Rows 2–6. Sk the first st, dc to the end. Ch1, turn.

Row 7. Sk the first st, 1dc. Fasten off. (1)

for the scoop of ice cream

Row 1. Using pink yarn, ch2 the work 3dc into the second ch from hook. Ch1, turn. (3)

Row 2. 2dc into every st. Ch1, turn. (6)

Row 3. *1dc, 2dc into the next st. Repeat from* twice. Ch1, turn. (9)

Row 4. *2dc, 2dc into the next st. Repeat from* twice. Ch1, turn. (12)

Row 5. *3dc, 2dc into the next st. Repeat from* twice. (15)

Fasten off leaving a 30cm tail. Thread the tail with a needle, run a gathering stitch along the base of the half circle.

Pull the thread to slightly gather in the base, sew to the top of the cone.

Glue to the ice cream truck and, stitch on a red bead. Repeat in lots of differ-ent flavours!

Make a quadruple scoop ice cream and glue it to the back. Position the red button at the top of the ice cream so that it not only represents a cherry, but also fits into the button loop on the roof.

for the ice lolly

Top

Foundation row. Using pink yarn, ch6.

Row 1. Starting from the 2nd ch from hook, 4dc, 3dc into the final ch. Work another 4dc along the opposite side of the ch. Ch1, turn. (11)

Row 2. 4dc, 2dc into each of the next 3sts, 4dc. Ch1, turn. (14)

Row 3. 5dc, 2dc into the next st, *1dc, 2dc into the next st. Repeat from * once more. 4dc, (1dc, ch1, 1dc) into the next st, 5dc across the base. Fasten off. (23)

lolly stick

Foundation row. Using beige yarn, ch4.

Row 1. Starting in the 2nd ch from hook, 3dc. Fasten off. (3)

Sew to the base of the ice lolly top.

Glue onto the ice cream truck, make some more!

for the blackboards

blackboard 1

This blackboard sits above the concession window.

Foundation row. Using black yarn, ch21.

Row 1. Starting from the 2nd ch from hook, 20dc. Ch1, turn. (20)

Rows 2–5. 1dc into every st. Ch1, turn.

Row 6. 1dc into every st. Fasten off.

Round 7. Change to beige yarn. 1dc into every st, (1dc, ch1, 1dc) into each corner. (52) Fasten off.

Embroider with mini ice creams and ice lollies (see photograph as a guide).

blackboard 2

Make 2

Position one on the back and one inside the truck.

Foundation row. Using black yarn, ch11.

Row 1. Starting from the 2nd ch from hook, 10dc. Ch1, turn. (10)

Rows 2–15. 1dc into every st. Ch1, turn.

Row 16. 1dc into every st. Fasten off.

Round 17. Change to beige yarn. 1dc into every st, (1dc, ch1, 1dc) into each corner. Fasten off. (52)

Embroider with mini ice creams and ice lollies (see photograph as a guide).

**for the teensy
tiny ice lollies**
pink 4ply yarn
2.5mm crochet hook
small piece of brown card stock

**for the teensy
tiny ice creams**
blue 4ply yarn
2.5mm crochet hook
small piece of brown card stock

for the ice lolly
Make 2
Foundation row. Using pink yarn and
a 2.5mm crochet hook, ch4.
Round 1. Starting from the 2nd ch from
hook, 3dc, 3dc into the last ch, 2dc along
the opposite side of the foundation ch. Ch1,
3dc along the base. (10)

Cut out a small strip of card for the stick.
Glue the stick to the inside of the ice lolly
so that the end pokes out from the base.

Sandwich the cardboard stick between the
two crocheted sections and stitch together.

for the cone
Foundation row. Using beige yarn and
a 2.5mm crochet hook, ch4.
Row 1. Starting in the 2nd ch from hook,
2dc, 1htr into the last ch. Ch2, turn. (3)
Row 2. 1htr, 1dc, ss into the final st.
Sew Rows 1 and 2 together to create a
little cone.

for the scoop of ice cream
Round 1. Using pale blue yarn, ch2, 6dc
into the second ch from hook, ss back into
the first dc.

Sew onto the top of the cone, slightly
pinching the circle so that it forms a ball.
Repeat in another colour to make it
a double or triple scoop!

chest freezer

for the chest freezer

pink 4ply yarn

silver 4ply yarn

2.5mm crochet hook

cardboard

duct tape

for the chest freezer

Note: Rows 1–16 will form inside the freezer.

Foundation row. Using silver yarn and a 2.5mm crochet hook, ch9.

Row 1. Starting from the 2nd ch from hook, 8dc. Ch1, turn. (8)

Rows 2–16. 1dc into every st. Ch1, turn.

Round 7. 1dc into every st around each side. (44)

Rounds 8–11. 1dc into every st.

Round 12. Working into BLO, 1dc into every st.

Round 13. 1dc into every st.

Rounds 14–21. Change to pink yarn. 1dc into every st.

Row 22. 8dc. Ch1, turn. (8)

Rows 23–36. 1dc into every st. Ch1, turn.

Row 37. 1dc into every st. Fasten off. Measure the base and cut a piece of cardboard to match.

Repeat with the sides, measuring from the base Round 12 where a ridge was made by working into BLO.

Cut out the corresponding sizes from cardboard.

Tape the sides and base together to form a rectangular box.

Insert the cardboard box into the freezer until it reaches the line from Round 12.

Push the inside of the freezer down into the top of the cardboard box.

Sew the base section to the sides.

for the chest freezer lid

Foundation row. Using pink yarn, ch9.

Round 1. Starting from the 2nd ch from hook, 7dc, 2dc into the last ch. Work 7dc along the opposite side of the foundation ch. (16)

Rounds 2–18. 1dc into every st. (16) Measure the lid, cut a piece of cardboard to match.

Insert the cardboard into the lid.

Sew up the open side of the lid.

Sew one side to the back of the chest freezer.

lakeside
memories

Back in the 1970s we had a holiday house. It was set in a coastal part of Victoria called the Gippsland Lakes and was only accessible by boat. A weatherboard cottage with a deep verandah, it was nestled into the sand dunes and flanked by tea trees. There was a small stretch of beach in front of the house with a long jetty that stretched from our front lawn out to the boat. I was only four when we sold it, and although I only have a few memories of it, they are strong: waking early one morning and running along the jetty to surprise my older brother and sister who had slept all night on the boat; getting prickles from the salt-roughened wood and being ferried about in our little sailboats. Making this scene recaptures so much of that time for me.

Patterns in this Section

Cabin	Bed and blanket
Jetty	Wood burner
Pot plants	Sailboat
Window box	Canoe
Floor rug	Lake mat

cabin

for the cabin

2 x 50g balls
charcoal black DK yarn

2 x 50g balls
rich cream DK yarn

2 x 50g balls silver 4ply yarn

pale cream DK yarn

teal green DK yarn

pale blue DK yarn

3.5mm crochet hook

cardboard

glue

lightweight cotton fabric such
as lawn, approx. 28 x
20cm

1 bead

small amount of lace

duct tape

craft knife

Yarn suggestion: Try using matt cotton for the cabin walls and floor to give the appearance of painted wood. While you can use silver DK yarn for the roof, I recommend using 2 balls of silver 4ply yarn held together as the leftover bits can be used in other patterns throughout the book that require silver 4ply yarn.

Note: I consider 'right side' of the cabin walls to be the side on which the FLO stitches are worked as I like the effect. Feel free to use whichever side you prefer.

for the external back and side wall

Foundation row. Starting at the bottom using charcoal black yarn and a 3.5mm crochet hook, ch78.

Row 1. Starting in 3rd ch from hook, 76htr. Ch2, turn. (76)

Row 2. 1htr into FLO of each st. Ch2, turn.

Row 3. 1htr into every st. Ch2, turn.

Repeat rows 2 and 3 until 14 rows in total have been worked. Fasten off.

for the internal back and side wall

Foundation row. Starting at the bottom and using rich cream yarn, ch74. Repeat the instructions for the external wall until Row 14, keeping in mind that this version is smaller by 4sts.

Row 14. 1dc into every st.

for the external front wall

Foundation row. Starting at the bottom and using charcoal black yarn, ch28.

Row 1. Starting in 3rd ch from hook, 26htr. Ch2, turn. (26)

This section is now worked in two parts (a and b) to create a gap for the front door.

Row 2a. Working into FLO, 8htr. Ch2, turn. (8)

Row 3a. 8htr. Ch2, turn.

Repeat rows 2a and 3a until 9 rows beginning from row 2a have been worked. Fasten off.

Rows 2b–9b. Working into Row 1, reattach the yarn leaving a 10 st gap for the door then work as for the first side.

Row 10b. Working into FLO, 8htr. Ch2, turn.

Row 11. 8htr, ch10 (across gap), 8htr (into section a). (16)

Row 12. Working into FLO, 8htr, 1htr into each ch, working into FLO, 8htr. Ch2, turn. (26)

Row 13. 1htr into every st. Ch2, turn.

Row 14. 1htr into FLO of each st. Fasten off.

Measure the external front wall and cut 4 pieces of cardboard to match.

for the internal front wall

Foundation row. Starting at the bottom and using rich cream yarn, ch26.

Repeat the instructions for the external wall to Row 14, keeping in mind that the internal front wall is smaller by 2sts, and working 7htr instead of 8htr on Rows 2–10.

Row 14. 1dc into every st. Fasten off.

for the external base

Foundation row. Using charcoal black yarn, ch26.

Row 1. Starting in 3rd ch from hook, 24htr. Ch2, turn. (24)

Row 2. 1htr into FLO of every st. Ch2, turn. (24)

Row 3. 1htr into every st. Ch2, turn. (24)

Repeat Rows 2–3 until 16 rows in total have been completed.

for the internal floor

Foundation row. Using rich cream yarn, ch25.

Row 1. Starting in 2nd ch from hook, 24dc. Ch1, turn. (24)

Rows 2–25. 1dc into every st. Ch1, turn.

Row 26. 1dc into every st. Fasten off.

to construct the cardboard cabin frame

Take the 4 cardboard walls and tape together to form a cube.

Measure the base and cut another piece to suit.

Tape the base to the walls (see the illustration on page 62).

to construct the cabin

Sew the two external panels together. Crochet 1dc around the bottom using pale cream yarn.

Sew the internal panels together.

Sew the internal base to the bottom of the internal walls.

Insert the internal section into the cardboard frame.

Insert the cardboard frame into the external walls.

Crochet the internal and external walls together by working 1dc into every stitch around the top using pale cream.

Sew the external base to the external walls.

Using the craft knife, cut out a section for the front door.

for the roof

Foundation row. Using two strands of silver yarn held together, ch44.
Row 1. Starting in 2nd ch from hook, 43dc. Ch1, turn. (43)
Rows 2–43. 1dc into every st. Ch1, turn.
Round 44. 1dc into every st around the entire roof. Fasten off. (170)

to construct the roof

Measure the length and width of the roof, reducing the measurements by 5mm around each side and cut a piece of cardboard to match.

The crocheted roof should have a corrugated iron effect. Bend the roof so that the corrugations run parallel down the roof (so that the 'rain' can run off).

Cut the cardboard template in half ensuring that the corrugation will sit along the roof in the right direction.

Lay one of the cardboard templates onto the fabric and cut out two fabric pieces, leaving a 1cm margin around the fabric.

Glue the fabric to the cardboard, wrapping the margin over to the back of the cardboard.

Glue the cardboard to the roof, with the crochet facing outward. Put to one side while you make the gables.

for the gables
Row 1. Using charcoal black yarn, ch2 then work 2 dc back into the 2nd ch from hook. Ch1, turn. (2)
Row 2. 2dc into each st. Ch1, turn. (4)
Row 3. 1dc, 2dc into each of the next 2 sts, 1dc. Ch1, turn. (6)
Row 4. 1dc into every st. Ch1, turn.
Rows 5–7. 1dc, 2dc in next st, dc across to the last 2 sts, 2dc into the next st, 1 dc. Ch1, turn.
Row 8. 1dc into every st. Ch1, turn. (12)
Rows 9–15. 1dc, 2dc in next st, dc across to the last 2 sts, 2dc into the next st, 1 dc.

Trace around the crochet piece onto cardboard and cut out two pieces to match. Set aside.
Row 16. 1dc into BLO of each st. Ch1, turn. (26)
Rows 17–23. 1dc, sk one st, dc across to the last 2sts, sk one st, 1dc. Ch1, turn.
Row 24. 1dc into every st. Ch1, turn. (12)
Rows 25–27. 1dc, sk one st, dc across to the last 2sts, sk one st, 1dc. Ch1, turn.
Row 28. 1dc into every st. Ch1, turn. (6)
Row 29. 1dc, sk one st, 2dc, sk one st, 1dc. Ch1, turn. (4)
Row 30. 1dc, sk the next 2sts, 1dc. Ch1, turn. (2)
Row 31. 1dc. Fasten off. (1)

Fold the two halves of the crochet piece together to make a triangle.

Sit the cardboard inside the triangle and sew together around the edges.

Run a line of thick PVA or hot glue around the two stitched sides of the gable.

Glue flush to the back end of the roof so that the gable forms a triangle.

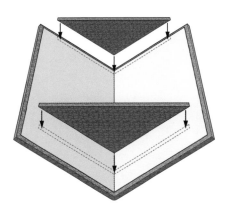

Sit the roof on top of the cabin to work out where the next gable should be positioned – leave an overhang over the front door to create a verandah. The roof should fit like a lid on top of the cabin.

Glue the second gable into place.

for the door

Foundation row. Using teal green yarn, ch16.
Row 1. Starting in 2nd ch from hook, 15dc. Ch1, turn. (15)
Rows 2–19. 1dc into every st. Ch1, turn.
Row 20. 1dc into every st. Fasten off.

Fold in half lengthways and make cardboard template to match.

Insert the cardboard template into the centre and stitch up the sides.

for the door frame

Using pale cream yarn, crochet a length of chain that is approximately 3cm longer than the length around the door frame.

Starting from the 2nd ch from hook, work 1dc along the length of the ch.
Sew the chain around the door frame with the two ends meeting at the centre bottom.

Sew the left-hand side of the door to the inside of the door frame.

Attach a bead for the door knob.

for the square window

Foundation row. Using pale blue yarn, ch12.
Row 1. Starting in 2nd ch from hook, 11dc. Ch1, turn. (11)
Rows 2–6. 1dc into every st. Ch1, turn.
Row 7. 1dc into every st. Fasten off.
Round 8. Using pale cream yarn, work 1dc into every st around each side and (1dc, ch2, 1dc) into every corner. (48)

Fasten off leaving a long tail to embroider window panes.

Embroider a series of lines as indicated by the photos to create 6 equal squares on the windows.

Glue the outside two windows into position on the side walls.

Sew a small amount of lace into each of the internal windows. Glue into place.

for the round window

Round 1. Using pale blue yarn, ch2, 6dc into the second ch from hook. Ss back into the first dc. (6)
Round 2. 2dc into every st. (12)
Round 3. *1dc, 2dc into the next st. Repeat from * until the end of the round. (18)
Round 4. Change to pale cream yarn. *2dc, 2dc into the next st. Repeat from* until the end of the round. (24)

Fasten off leaving a long tail to embroider, window panes.

Embroider two lines in the window to create a cross.

Glue into position on the external front gable.

jetty

Make 2

Foundation row. Using brown yarn and a 3.5mm crochet hook, ch11.

Row 1. Starting in 2nd ch from hook, 10dc. Ch1, turn. (10)
Rows 2–25. 1dc into every st. Ch1, turn. (10)
Row 26. 1dc into every st. Fasten off.

Measure the length and width of the jetty and cut a piece of cardboard to match.

Sandwich the cardboard between the two crochet pieces and sew together.

Using the hot glue gun, glue the dowels, 3 on each side, into place.

If you do not have dowels, cut coloured pencils into 3cm lengths or roll up lengths of card stock instead.

pot plants

for the pot
Make 2

Round 1. Using tan yarn and a 2.5mm crochet hook, ch2, 6dc into the second ch from hook. Ss back into the first dc. (6)

Round 2. 2dc into every st. (12)

Round 3. *1dc, 2dc into the next st. Repeat from * until the end of the round. (18)

Round 4. 1dc into BLO of every st.

Rounds 5–6. 1dc into every st.

Round 7. *5dc, 2dc into the next st. Repeat from * until the end of the round. (21)

Rounds 8–10. 1dc into every st.

Round 11. 1dc into FLO of every st.

Round 12. 1dc into every st. Fasten off.

Fold the last round over to the outside to create a lip and sew into place. Stuff lightly.

for the greenery
Make 2

Foundation row. Using green yarn and a 3.5mm hook, ch50.

Row 1. 1ss into the fourth ch from hook. *Ch3 then ss into the next st. Repeat from * until the end of the foundation ch. Fasten off leaving a tail.

Bunch the greenery chain up and sew into a bundle using the tail.

for the hydrangea flower
Make enough to decorate both pots.

Round 1. Using lilac yarn and a 2.5mm hook, ch2, 6dc into the 2nd ch from hook, ss back into the first dc.

Decorate with French knots in blue yarn (see page 15).

Sew the hydrangea onto the greenery bundle and then use the tail to sew French knots onto the greenery.

Make more hydrangeas, alternating the lilac and the blue for the hydrangea base.
Sew the hydrangea plant onto the pot.

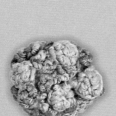
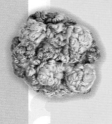

window box

for the window box

tan 4ply yarn

green DK yarn

red 4ply yarn

2.5mm crochet hook

3.5mm crochet hook

embroidery needle

cardboard

for the box
Make 2
Foundation row. Using tan yarn and a 2.5mm crochet hook, ch17.
Row 1. Starting in 2nd ch from hook, 16dc. Ch1, turn. (16)
Rows 2–3. 1dc into every st. Ch1, turn. (16)
Round 4. 1dc into every st around each side. (34)

Fasten off leaving a long tail to stitch the greenery to the inside of the window box.

Trace around the bottom of the window box (the section worked in rows) and cut a piece of cardboard to match.

Place the cardboard in the bottom of the window box. This will keep it in shape.

for the greenery
Foundation Row. Using green yarn and a 3.5mm hook, ch31.
Row 1. 1ss into the fourth ch from hook. *Ch3 then ss into the next st. Repeat from * until the end of the foundation ch.

Stuff the greenery into the window box and sew into position.

Using the red yarn and an embroidery needle, cover the greenery with French knots (see page 15), wrapping the needle 2–4 times to vary the size of the flower.

floor rug

for the floor rug

yellow 4ply yarn

pale blue 4ply yarn

red 4ply yarn

pink 4ply yarn

cream 4ply yarn

2.5mm crochet hook

bed and blanket

for the bed and blanket

yellow 4ply yarn

2.5mm crochet hook

cardboard

wadding

for the floor rug

Foundation Row. Using yellow yarn and a 2.5mm crochet hook, ch7.

Round 1. Starting in 2nd ch from hook, 5dc, 2dc into the final ch, 5dc along the opposite side of the foundation ch.

Round 2. Change to pale blue yarn. 3dc into the first st, 5dc, 3dc into the next st, 5dc. (16)

Round 3. *2dc into each of the next 3 sts, 5dc. Repeat from * once more. (22)

Round 4. Change to red yarn. *1dc, 2dc into the next st. Repeat from * two more times. 5dc. *1dc then 2dc into the next st. Repeat from * two more times. 5dc. (28)

Round 5. *2dc, 2dc into the next st. Repeat from * two more times. 5dc. *2dc then 2dc into the next st. Repeat from * two more times. 5dc. (34)

Round 6. Change to pink yarn. *3dc, 2dc into the next st. Repeat from * two more times. 5dc. *3dc, 2dc into the next st. Repeat from * two more times. 5dc. (40)

Round 5. *4dc, 2dc into the next st. Repeat from * two more times. 5dc. *4dc, 2dc into the next st. Repeat from * two more times. 5dc. (46)

Round 6. Change to cream yarn. *5dc, 2dc into the next st. Repeat from * two more times. 5dc. *5dc, 2dc into the next st. Repeat from * two more times. 5dc. Fasten off. (52)

for the blanket

Foundation row. Starting from the base of the blanket using yellow yarn and a 2.5mm crochet hook, ch13.

Row 1. 2tr into the 4th ch from hook, sk one st, ss into the next st, sk one st, *5tr into the next st, sk one st, ss into the following st. Repeat from * one more time. Ch3, turn.

Row 2. 2tr back into the first st, sk 2sts, ss into the following st, *sk 2sts, 5tr into the next st, sk 2sts, ss into the following st. Repeat from * one more time. Ch3, turn. Repeat row 2 until 9 rows in total have been completed. At the end of the last row, ch1 but do not turn.

Round 10. Work 13dc down the first side, (1dc, ch2 1dc) into the corner, 8dc, (1dc, ch2, 1dc) into the corner, 13dc. Ss into the top of the ch3 from the previous row. Fasten off.

for the bed

Follow the instructions for constructing the bed in the Caravan pattern on page 37 and the frame in the Canal Boat pattern on page 96.

wood burner

for the
wood burner

black DK yarn

silver 4ply yarn

3.5mm crochet hook

embroidery threads in
red and orange

embroidery needle

cardboard

stuffing

bamboo skewer

for the box

Foundation row. Beginning from the base, using black yarn and a 3.5mm crochet hook, ch6.

Row 1. Starting in 2nd ch from hook, 5dc. Ch1, turn. (5)

Rows 2–5. 1dc into every st. Ch1, turn. (5)

Round 6. 1dc into every st around each side of the square. (18)

Rounds 7–12. 1dc into every st.

Row 13. 1dc into BLO into the next 5sts. Ch1, turn. (5)

Rows 14–16. 1dc into every st. Ch1, turn.

Row 17. 1dc into every st. Fasten off.

Cut two small squares of cardboard and place one in the bottom of the box.

Stuff then place the other cardboard square on top.

Sew down the top of the box.

for the door

Foundation row. Using black yarn, ch5.

Row 1. Starting in 2nd ch from hook, 4dc. Ch1, turn. (4)

Rows 2–3. 1dc into every st. Ch1, turn. (4)

Row 4. 1dc into every st. Fasten off. (4)

Round 5. Using silver yarn, work 1dc into every st and (1dc, ch2, 1dc) into each corner. Fasten off. (18)

Embroider the flames using red and orange embroidery thread making a series of fanning lines in straight stitch.

Sew the door onto the box.

for the chimney

Foundation row. Using black yarn, ch16.

Row 1. Starting in 2nd ch from hook, 15dc. Ch1, turn. (15)

Row 2. 1dc into every st. Ch1, turn. (15)

Row 3. 1dc into every st. Fasten off. (15)

Cut a bamboo skewer to match the length of the chimney.

Place the skewer on top of the strip of crochet and then sew the edges and ends together.

Sew to the top of the box.

Have some fun decorating your cabin. I stuck a vintage card with an insect onto the wall with glue. You could use bunting (see pages 14 and 28), or make a line of windows along the back. You could attach a tiny washing line and hang up miniature towels and clothes to dry!

saliboat

for the sailboat

yellow DK yarn

cream DK yarn

blue DK yarn

3.5mm crochet hook

lightweight fabric such as lawn, approx. 15 x 15cm

fine wire

cotton sewing thread and needle

decorative paper

drinking straw

for the external layer

Row 1. Beginning at the base, using yellow yarn and a 3.5mm crochet hook, starting in 2nd ch from hook, 1dc. Ch1, turn. (1)

Row 2. 3dc into the first st. Ch1, turn. (3)

Row 3. 2dc into the first st, 1dc, 2dc into the last st. Ch1, turn. (5)

Rows 4–5. 1dc, 2dc into the next st, dc across to the last 2 sts, 2dc into the next st, 1 dc. Ch1, turn.

Row 6. 1dc into every st. Ch1, turn. (9)

Row 7. 1dc, 2dc into the next st, 7dc, 2dc into the next st, 1dc. Ch1, turn. (11)

Rows 8–18. 1dc into every st. Ch1, turn.

Row 19. 1dc, sk one st, 7dc, sk one st, 1dc. Ch1, turn. (9)

Row 20. 1dc into every st. Ch1, turn.

Rows 21–23. 1dc, sk one st, dc across to the last 2 sts, sk one st, 1dc. Ch1, turn.

Row 24. 1dc, sk one st, 1dc. Ch1, turn. (2)

Row 25. 1dc. Ch1. (1)

Round 26. 23dc down the side of the base (created by rows 1–25). 2dc into the last st. 23dc down the opposite side. (48)

Round 27. 2dc into the first st, 46dc, 2dc into the last st. (50)

Round 28. 24dc, 2dc into each of the following 2sts, 24dc. (52)

Round 29. 1dc into every st until the end of the round. (52)

Round 30. 2dc into the first st. 50dc. 2dc into the last st. (54)

for the internal layer

Using cream yarn, repeat instructions as for the external layer up to Row 26 but sk one row between Rows 8–18 so that 10 rows are worked rather than 11.

Round 26. 22dc down the side of the base. 2dc into the last st. 22dc down the opposite side. (46)

Round 27. 2dc into the first st, 44dc, 2dc into the last st. (48)

Round 28. 23dc, 2dc into each of the following 2sts, 23dc. (50)

Round 29. 2dc into the first st. 48dc. 2dc into the last st. (52)

Insert the internal layer into the external layer and crochet together as follows:

Using cream yarn, 26dc, 2dc into each of the next 2sts, 26dc, ss back into the first dc. Fasten off. (56)

for the mast step

Foundation row. Using yellow yarn, ch4.

Row 1. 1dc into the 2nd st from hook. Work 2dc along the foundation ch. (3)

Rows 2–3. 1dc into every st. Ch1, turn. (3)

Row 4. 1dc into every st. Ch3, ss back into the first dc of the row. (3)

Round 5. 2dc into each of the next 3sts, 2dc into ch across the 3chsp. (12)

Round 6. *1dc then 2dc into the next st. Repeat from * until the end of the round. (18) Fasten off.

Make three cuts into the bottom of a paper straw, 1cm long.

Insert the straw up through the hole of the mast step.

Flare out the bottom of the straw so that it sits under the mast step.

Sew the edges of Rows 1–3 together so that the straw sits firmly inside.

Sew the mast step to the inside of the boat at the bow (see the photo on page 73).

for the sail

Cut a triangle of fabric approximately 14cm along the base by 13.5cm on the two sides.

Fold in half, right side in, and either hand or machine stitch down the diagonal edge.

Turn the fabric right side out.

Cut a piece of fine wire so that it is the same length as the three edges of the fabric triangle.

Shape the wire into a triangle and twist the ends together.

Insert into the base of the sail. Sew the bottom of the sail together.

Either baste to the mast or glue approximately 4cm above the bottom of the boat.

Cut off the excess straw above the sail.

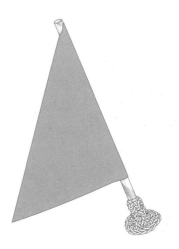

canoe

for the canoe

yellow DK yarn

rich cream DK yarn

tan 4ply yarn

3.5mm crochet hook

2.5mm crochet hook

bamboo skewer

washi tape

glue

for the external layer

Foundation row. Using yellow yarn and a 3.5mm crochet hook, ch23.

Round 1. Starting in 2nd ch from hook, 21dc, 2dc into the final ch, 21dc along the opposite side of the ch. (44)

Round 2. 2dc into the first st, 42dc, 2dc into the last st. (46)

Round 3. 22dc, 2dc into each of the following 2sts, 22dc. (48)

Round 4. 1dc into every st.

Round 5. 2dc into the first st, 46dc, 2dc into the last st. (50)

Round 6. 24dc, 2dc into each of the following 2sts, 24dc. (52)

for the internal layer

Foundation row: Using rich cream yarn and a 3.5mm crochet hook, ch22.

Round 1. Starting in 2nd ch from hook, 20dc, 2dc into the final ch. Work 20dc along the opposite side of the ch. (42)

Round 2. 2dc into the first st, 40dc, 2dc into the last st. (44)

Round 3. 21dc, 2dc into each of the following 2sts, 21dc. (46)

Round 4. 2dc into the first st, 44dc, 2dc into the last st. (48)

Round 5. 23dc, 2dc into each of the following 2sts, 23dc. (50)

Rounds 6–7. Insert the internal layer into the external layer and crochet together using rich cream yarn. 2dc into the first st, 50dc, 2dc into the last st. (54)

Sew the first 7 sts together at either end. Pinch into shape.

for the paddle

Make 2, one for each end of the skewer.
Foundation row. Using tan yarn and
a 2.5mm crochet hook. Ch4.

Round 1. Starting in 2nd ch from hook 2dc,
2dc into the last st. Work 2dc along the
opposite side of the foundation ch. (6)
Rounds 2–4. 1dc into every st. Fasten off.

Cover a bamboo skewer with washi tape
(see page 14) and cut to a suitable length
for the paddle.

Dip the end of the skewer in glue then insert
halfway into the crochet paddle.

Sew up either side of the top of the paddle
so that the skewer sits firmly inside.

Flatten the end of the paddle.

Repeat with the other end
of the paddle.

lake mat

for the lake mat

3 x 50g balls of
grass green DK yarn

4 x 50g balls
of pale blue DK yarn

2 x 50g balls of
dark green DK yarn

3.5mm crochet hook

cardboard

wadding

Yarn suggestion: For contrasting textures between the lake and grass, I would suggest wool for the lawn and a bamboo/wool mix for the water. To avoid any problems that may occur with yarns of slightly different tension, the water section is worked to the length of the lawn rather than by the number of rows.

for the lawn

Foundation row. Using grass green yarn, ch68.
Row 1. Starting in 3rd ch from hook, 66htr. Ch1, turn. (66)
Rows 2–65. 1htr into every st. Ch1, turn.
Row 66. 1htr into every st. Fasten off.

for the water

Foundation row. Using pale blue yarn, ch73.
Row 1. 2tr into the 4th ch from hook (this counts as 3tr), sk 2sts, 1dc into the next st, *sk 2sts, 5tr into the following st, sk 2sts, 1dc into the next st. Repeat from * until the final st. Ch3, turn.
Row 2. 2tr into the last dc from the previous row, sk 2sts, 1dc into the next st (top centre of the 5tr cluster from the last row). *Sk 2sts, 5tr into the following dc, sk 2sts, 1dc into the next st. Repeat from * until the final st. Ch3, turn.
Repeat Row 2 until water measures 1 row fewer than the length of the grass section and end with ch2.

Work the following instructions to change the scalloped edge into a straight edge:
Side 1 (Row 1). 2htr into the first dc, *ch1, sk 2sts, 1dc into the next st (top centre of the 5tr from the last row), ch1, sk the next 2 sts, 3htr into the next dc. Repeat from * until the end of the row ending with a dc. Ch1, turn.
Side 1 (Row 2). 1dc into the first st, 2dc into the 1chsp, 2dc into the top middle of the 3htr from the previous row. *2dc into every 1chsp, 2dc into the top of each 3tr cluster. Repeat from * until the end of the side. (1dc, ch2, 2dc) into the corner st.
Side 2. 1dc into the next st, *2dc along the ch3 from the tr cluster, 1dc into the base of the ch3. Repeat from * until the end of the side. (2dc, ch2, 1dc) into the corner st.
Side 3. 1dc into the next st, *2dc into the ch2 gap, 1dc into the next st (where 1dc

was worked into the foundation ch in Row 1), 2dc into the ch2 gap, 1dc into the next st (where 5tr were worked into the foundation ch in Row 1). Repeat from * until the end of the side. (2dc, ch2, 1dc) into the corner st.
Side 4. 1dc into the next st, *2dc along the ch3 from the tr cluster, 1dc into the base of the ch3. Repeat from * until the end of the side. (1dc, ch2, ss into the next st) into the corner st. Fasten off.

for the half circle bank
Make one large and one small.
Row 1. Using dark green yarn, ch2, 3dc into the 2nd ch from hook. Ch1, turn. (3)
Row 2. 2dc into each st. Ch1, turn. (6)
Row 3. *1dc, 2dc into the next st. Repeat from * twice. Ch1, turn. (9)
Row 4. *2dc, 2dc into the next st. Repeat from * twice. Ch1, turn. (12)
Row 5. *3dc, 2dc into the next st. Repeat from * twice. Ch1, turn. (15)
Row 6. *4dc, 2dc into the next st. Repeat from * twice. Ch1, turn. (18)

Row 7. *5dc, 2dc into the next st. Repeat from * twice. Ch1, turn. (21)
Row 8. *6dc, 2dc into the next st. Repeat from * twice. Ch1, turn. (24)
Row 9. *7dc, 2dc into the next st. Repeat from * twice. Ch1, turn. (27)
Row 10. *8dc, 2dc into the next st. Repeat from * twice. Ch1, turn. (30)

for small bank only
Round 11. 1dc into every st. Fasten off. (50)

for large bank only
Row 11. *9dc, 2dc into the next st. Repeat from * twice. Ch1, turn. (33)
Row 12. *10dc, 2dc into the next st. Repeat from * twice. Ch1, turn. (36)
Row 13. *11dc, 2dc into the next st. Repeat from * twice. Ch1, turn. (39)
Row 14. *12dc, 2dc into the next st. Repeat from * twice. Ch1, turn. (42)
Round 15. 1dc into every st. Fasten off. (70)

for the quarter circle bank
Row 1. Using dark green yarn, ch2, 1dc into the 2nd ch from hook. Ch1, turn. (1)
Row 2. 2dc into the same st. Ch1, turn. (2)
Row 3. 2dc into each st. Ch1, turn. (4)
Row 4. *1dc, 2dc into the next st. Repeat from * once more. Ch1, turn. (6)
Rows 5–17. 1dc, 2dc into the next st, dc across to the last 2sts, 2dc into the next st, 1 dc. Ch1, turn. (32)
Round 18. 1dc into every st (16dc down each straight side). Fasten off. (64)

Trace around all the banks and cut out pieces of cardboard to match.

Sew into place so that their flat edges line up with the outer perimeter of the water.

for the island

Round 1. Using dark green yarn, ch2, 6dc into the 2nd ch from hook, ss back into the first dc. (6)

Round 2. 2dc into each st. (12)

Round 3. *1dc, 2dc into the next st. Repeat from * until the end of the round. (18)

Round 4. *2dc, 2dc into the next st. Repeat from * until the end of the round. (24)

Round 5. *3dc, 2dc into the next st. Repeat from * until the end of the round. (30)

Round 6. *4dc, 2dc into the next st. Repeat from * until the end of the round. (36)

Round 7. *5dc, 2dc into the next st. Repeat from * until the end of the round. (42)

Round 8. *6dc, 2dc into the next st. Repeat from * until the end of the round. (48)

Round 9. *7dc, 2dc into the next st. Repeat from * until the end of the round. (54)

Round 10. *8dc, 2dc into the next st. Repeat from * until the end of the round. (60)

Round 11. *9dc, 2dc into the next st. Repeat from * until the end of the round. (66)

Round 12. *10dc, 2dc into the next st. Repeat from * until the end of the round. (72)

Round 13. *11dc, 2dc into the next st. Repeat from * until the end of the round. (78)

Round 14. *12dc, 2dc into the next st. Repeat from * until the end of the round. (84)

Round 15. 1dc into every st. Fasten off. (84)

Trace around the island and cut out 1 piece of cardboard and 2 pieces of wadding to match.

Place the wadding flat inside the crochet and sandwich with the cardboard.

Sew onto the water.

to finish the lake

Sew the lawn and water sections together.

Round 1. Using dark green yarn, work 1dc into every st on each side and (1dc, ch2, 1dc) into every corner, ss back into the first dc.

Round 2. *Ch3, sk one st, ss into the next st. Repeat from* until the end of the round.

Fasten off.

canal boat
idyll

One of my many daydreams involves floating along a river in a beautiful canal boat, able to speak the language of any country that we drift through. Our whole family would be wearing matching striped Breton tops with jaunty scarves tied at an angle around our necks. I just know that my boys would love this (can you imagine…). I would sit on the roof with a sketchpad drawing wildflowers and rabbits. We would stop for every meal at a hidden gem where only one amazing dish would be served. I could go on but I suspect that this book would run out of pages. In the meantime, a canal boat for my mantelpiece will have to do.

Patterns in this Section

Boat base
Cabin
Life preserver
Blanket
Room divider
Pot plants
Bed and bench

canal boat

Yarn suggestion: A bamboo/wool mix yarn works wonderfully well in this project as its sheen makes the boat look as though it has just had a fresh coat of paint.

Special stitch: 3tr together (3tr tog)
This is very similar to a cluster stitch and is used to reduce the number of treble crochets in a row. Wrap the yarn around the hook, insert the hook through the stitch and grab the yarn. Draw the hook back through the stitch and then grab the yarn again. Pull the yarn through the first two stitches. *Wrap the yarn around the hook again and insert the hook through the next stitch. Grab the yarn and draw the hook back through the stitch again. Pull the yarn through the first two stitches. Repeat from * one more time then grab the yarn and pull it through all four of the loops left on the hook.

for the boat base
Foundation row. Using navy blue yarn and a 3.5mm crochet hook, ch19.
Row 1. Starting in 2nd ch from hook, 18dc. Ch1, turn. (18)
Rows 2–60. 1dc into every st. Ch1, turn.
Rows 61–62. 1dc, sk one st, dc across to the last st, sk one st, 1dc. Ch1, turn. (14)

Row 63. 1dc into every st. Ch1, turn.
Rows 64–69. Repeat Rows 61–63 twice more. (12)
Row 70. As for Row 61. (4)
Row 71. 1dc, sk the next 2sts, 1dc. Ch1.

Trace around the crochet base panel onto cardboard. Cut out two cardboard templates.

Round 72. 71dc down the first side, 17dc across the back, 71dc up the other side, ss back into the first dc. (159)
Rounds 73–76. 1dc into every st.
Round 77. Change to pink yarn. 1dc into every st.
Round 78. Change to sea green yarn. 1dc into every st.
Rounds 79–80. 1dc into every st.
Round 81. 1dc, sk one st, 10dc, sk one st, 27dc, sk one st, 30dc, sk one st, 16dc, sk one st, 30dc, sk one st, 27dc, sk one st, 9dc, sk one st, 1dc. (151)
Round 82. 1dc into every st.
Round 83. Change to pale blue yarn, working into BLO, 1dc into every st.
Rounds 83–90. 1dc into every st.
Round 91. Ch3, 3tr tog, 63tr, 3tr tog, 13tr, 3tr tog, 63tr, 3tr tog, ss back into the first ch3. Fasten off. (143)

for the canal boat
1 x 50g ball of navy blue DK yarn

1 x 50g ball of sea green DK yarn

1x 50g ball of pale blue DK yarn

pink DK yarn

3.5mm crochet hook

3 x paper drinking straws

cardboard

duct tape

craft knife

hot glue gun

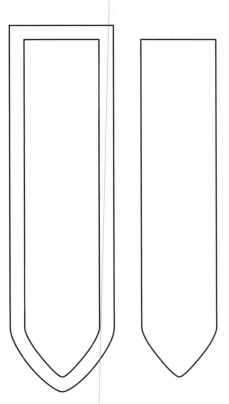

to construct the cardboard base frame

Measure the width from the beginning of Round 81 to the end of Round 82 (it should be approximately 1cm).

Take one cardboard base template and trace this margin around the inside of the template.

Using a craft knife, carefully cut around the margin to create two intact pieces – one outer ring, one inner piece. Measure the width between Rows 72–80.

Take the other base template. Now make the following three measurements: the length down either side of the base and the length across the straight end of the base.

Cut three pieces of cardboard to these lengths and the width between Rows 72–80.

Gently bend the sides of the longer pieces of cardboard to suit the curve of the base. Tape them together and repeat with the straight end.

Measure between the gap inside the base frame from the bottom to the top. Cut lengths of paper straws to fit and tape them inside. This gives the top rim more strength.

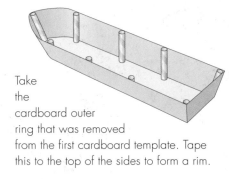

Take the cardboard outer ring that was removed from the first cardboard template. Tape this to the top of the sides to form a rim.

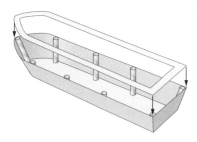

Take the leftover inner piece of cardboard and trace around it onto fabric, adding an extra 1cm margin on the outside.

Glue the fabric onto the cardboard, snip around the depth of the margin on the curves and then fold over and glue the margin to the back of the cardboard. Insert the cardboard base frame into the crochet base.

Stretch the sides around the cardboard frame and then down into the frame. Secure the inside edge of the crochet (Round 91) with little dabs of hot glue.

Glue the fabric covered cardboard base to the base frame making sure that the crocheted edges from Round 91 are covered.

Measure between the gap inside the base frame from the bottom to the top. Cut lengths of paper straws to fit and tape them inside. This gives the top rim more strength.

for the back flap

This section forms a platform between the back door of the cabin and the back of the boat base. The Captain does need somewhere to stand after all!

Foundation row. Using sea green yarn, ch15.
Row 1. Starting in 2nd ch from hook, 14dc. Ch1, turn. (14)
Row 2. 1dc into every st. Ch1, turn.
Row 3. 1dc into every st. Fasten off.

Sew to the edge of the BLO rim along the straight back end.

Sew the ends of the step to both sides of the rim.

cabin

for the cabin

2 x 50g balls of dusty yellow DK yarn

sky blue DK yarn

red DK yarn

pale blue 4ply yarn

silver 4ply yarn

3.5mm crochet hook

2.5mm crochet hook

cardboard

lightweight cotton fabric, approx. 45 x 40cm

duct tape

mini bobble trim or ricrac

1 x bead

fabric glue

hot glue gun

for the side panel

Foundation row. Using dusty yellow yarn and a 3.5mm crochet hook, ch13.
Row 1. Starting in 2nd ch from hook, 12dc. Ch1, turn. (12)
Rows 2–121. 1dc into every st. Ch1, turn.
Row 122. 1dc into every st. Fasten off.

Measure a length of cardboard to match the side panel.

Cut out a piece of fabric using the cardboard template, adding an extra 1cm margin to the piece.

Glue the fabric to the cardboard template, then fold and glue the extra margin of fabric around to the back of the cardboard template.

Establish where the template will need to bend for the back wall and lightly score the backside of the cardboard template in those places.

Glue the cardboard template to the crochet panel.

for the front panel

Foundation row. Using dusty yellow yarn and a 3.5mm crochet hook, ch20.
Row 1. Starting in 2nd ch from hook, 19dc. Ch1, turn. (19)
Rows 2–11. 1dc into every st. Ch1, turn.
Row 12. 1dc into every st. Fasten off.

Measure a length of cardboard to match the front panel.

Cut out a piece of fabric using the cardboard template, adding an extra 1cm margin to the piece.

Glue the fabric to the cardboard template and fold and glue the extra margin of fabric around to the back of the cardboard template.

Glue the cardboard template to crochet panel.

Sew the front panel to the two ends of the side panel.

for the roof

Foundation row. Using dusty yellow yarn and a 3.5mm crochet hook, ch14.
Row 1. Starting in 2nd ch from hook, 13dc. Ch1, turn. (13)
Rows 2–51. 1dc into every st. Ch1, turn.
Row 52. 1dc, sk one st, 11dc. Ch1, turn. (12)
Row 53. 1dc into every st. Ch1, turn.
Row 54. 10dc, sk one st, 1dc. Ch1, don't turn. (11)
Row 55. 53dc down the first side, (1dc, ch2, 1dc) into the corner st, 11dc. (1dc, ch2, 1dc) into the corner st, 53dc, ch2, ss back into the first dc. (121)
Round 56. Using sky blue yarn, 1dc into every st.
Fasten off.

Measure a length of cardboard to match the side panel.

Cut out a piece of fabric using the cardboard template, adding an extra 1cm margin to the piece.

Glue the fabric to the cardboard template and fold and glue the extra margin of fabric around to the back of the cardboard template.

Glue the cardboard template to crochet panel.

Sew one side of the roof to the side panel. Glue mini bobble trim around the top front and side panels.

for the door

Foundation row. Using red yarn and a 3.5mm crochet hook, ch8.
Row 1. Starting in 2nd ch from hook, 7dc. Ch1, turn. (7)
Rows 2–8. 1dc into every st. Ch1, turn.
Row 9. 1dc into every st. Fasten off.
Round 10. Using sky blue yarn, 1dc into every st around each side, (1dc, ch2, 1dc) into every corner st. (32)

Glue to the outside back wall of the cabin. Sew on a bead for a door knob.

for the rectangular windows

Make 12
Foundation row. Using pale blue yarn and a 2.5mm crochet hook, ch9.

Row 1. Starting in 2nd ch from hook, 8dc. Ch1, turn. (8)
Rows 2–6. 1dc into every st. Ch1, turn.
Row 7. 1dc into every st. Fasten off.
Round 8. Using silver yarn, work 1dc into every st around each side, (1dc, ch2, 1dc) into every corner st. (32)

Glue into place on the inside and outside of the cabin using photos as a guide.

for the round windows

Make 8
Round 1. Using pale blue yarn and a 2.5mm crochet hook, ch2. Work 6dc into the 2nd ch from hook, ss back into the first dc.
Round 2. 2dc into every st. (12)
Round 3. *1dc, 2dc into the next st. Repeat from * until the end of the round. (18)
Round 4. Using silver yarn. *2dc, 2dc into the next st.* Repeat until the end of the round. Fasten off. (24)

Glue into place on the inside and outside of the cabin following the photographs.

for the front window

Make 2

Foundation row. Using pale blue yarn and a 2.5mm crochet hook, ch9.

Row 1. Starting in 2nd ch from hook, 8dc Ch1, turn. (8)

Rows 2–13. 1dc into every st. Ch1, turn.

Row 14. 1dc into every st. Fasten off.

Round 15. Using silver yarn, 1dc into every st around each side, (1dc, ch2, 1dc) into every corner st. (46)

Glue into place on the inside and outside of the cabin following the photograph.

joining the base and the cabin

Run a fine line of hot glue around the bottom of the cabin and the line inside the base rim.

Place the cabin on top of the base so that the back of the cabin lines up with the back flap.

Hold firmly until the glue sets.
Sew the back flap along the bottom of the cabin (under the door).

life preserver

Round 1. Using red yarn and a 2.5mm crochet hook, ch18, ss back into the first st. Ch1, 1dc into every ch until the end of the round. (18)

Round 2. *2dc, 2dc into the next st. Repeat from * until the end of the round. (24)

Round 3. *3dc, 2dc into the next st. Repeat from * until the end of the round. (30)

Round 4. *4dc, 2dc into the next st. Repeat from * until the end of the round. (36)

Round 5. *5dc, sk the next st. Repeat from * until the end of the round. (30)

Round 6. *4dc then sk the next st. Repeat from * until the end of the round. (24)

Round 4. *3dc, sk the next st. Repeat from * until the end of the round. (18)

Fasten off, leaving a long tail for stitching up the central hole.

to construct the life preserver

Lay the crochet piece on top of cardboard and trace around the inner and outer circles.

Cut out the large circle and then, using a craft knife, carefully remove the central hole.

Insert the cardboard template into the crochet life preserver.

Sew the two inside edges together. Using the cream yarn, wrap the yarn around 3 equal sections of the life preserver as shown in the photograph. It works best to fasten off between each stripe.

Using the tan yarn, make a knot on the edge in between two of the cream stripes and then run the yarn around the outside edge of the life preserver, knotting it into the preserver at five other equal points. Sew to the side of the canal boat.

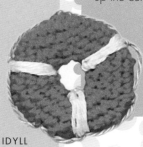

blanket

for the blanket
green 4ply yarn
royal blue 4ply yarn
2.5mm crochet hook

Work the blanket in the following colour-way by alternating two rows in green with two rows of royal blue.

Foundation row. Using green yarn and a 2.5mm crochet hook, ch11.
Row 1. Starting in 2nd ch from hook, 10dc. Ch1, turn. (10)
Rows 2–13. 1dc into every st. Ch1, turn.
Row 14. 1dc into every st. Fasten off.
Round 15. Using royal blue yarn, 1dc into every st around each side, (1dc, ch2, 1dc) into every corner st. (50).
Round 16. *3dc into the first st, sk one st, ss into the following st. Repeat from * until the end of the round.
Fasten off.

room divider

for the room divider/trunk

silver 4ply yarn
turquoise 4ply yarn
2.5mm crochet hook
cardboard
duct tape

Note: Rows 1–18 will form the inside of the trunk.

Foundation row. Using silver yarn and a 2.5mm crochet hook, ch6.
Row 1. Starting in 2nd ch from hook, 5dc. Ch1, turn. (5)
Rows 2–13. 1dc into every st. Ch1, turn.
Rounds 14–18. 1dc into every st around each side. (34)
Round 19. Working into BLO, 1dc into every st.
Rounds 20–24. 1dc into every st each side. (34)
Round 25. As Round 19
Rounds 26–27. 1dc into every st.
Rounds 28–37. Change to turquoise yarn, 1dc into every st.
Row 38. 5dc. Ch1, turn. (5)
Rows 39–50. 1dc into each st. Ch1, turn. (5)
Row 51. 1dc into each st. Fasten off.
Follow the construction method given for the chest freezer pattern on page 56.

for the lid

Foundation row. Using silver yarn, ch7.
Row 1. Starting in 2nd ch from hook, 5dc, 2dc into the last ch, 5dc along the opposite side of the foundation ch. (12)
Rows 2–14. 1dc into every st.

Follow the construction method given for the chest freezer pattern on page 56.

pot plants

for the pot plants
tan 4ply yarn
4ply yarn in assorted colours
for flowers
4ply green yarn in assorted tones
2.5mm crochet hook
3.5mm crochet hook
stuffing
embroidery needle

for the pot

Round 1. Using tan yarn and a 2.5mm crochet hook, ch2. Work 6dc into the second ch from hook, ss back into the first dc.
Round 2. 2dc into every st. (12)
Round 3. Working into BLO, 1dc into every st. (12)
Rounds 4. 1dc into every st. (12)
Round 5. *3dc then 2dc into the next st. Repeat from * twice. (15)
Round 6. 1dc into every st. (15)
Round 7. Working into FLO, *4dc then 2dc into the next st. Repeat from * until the end of the round.

Fasten off, leaving a long tail for stitching the plant in place. (18)

for the wood burner

Follow the instructions from the Lakeside Cabin pattern (see page 72), apart from the chimney. Instead ch11 and work 9dc along the foundation ch.

for the plant

Foundation row. Using green yarn and a 3.5mm crochet hook, ch20.
Row 1. Ss into the 4th ch from hook, *ch3, ss into the next st. Repeat from * until the end of the foundation ch.

Bunch the greenery chain up and sew into a little bundle.

Using one of the 4ply coloured yarns, embroider French knots over the greenery, wrapping the needle 4–5 times with the yarn (see page 15).

Fill the pot with a small amount of stuffing then sew the plant into place.

For further pot plants, vary the foundation chain length to give the effect of different types of plants.

French knots clustered in the centre of the plant is a great way to create a whole new plant! Pop a hydrangea pot into the bow (front deck).

bed + bench

for the bed and bench

yellow 4ply yarn

2.5mm crochet hook

wadding

cardboard

decorative paper drinking straws

washi tape

bamboo skewers

needle

hot glue gun

Follow the instructions from the Caravan pattern for the bed and bench, cushions and pillows on pages 37–38, and then make the frames in the following way:

for the bed frame

Cut two 7cm pieces of straw.

Bend at 2cm in on either side.

Cut two 3cm pieces of bamboo skewers and cover with washi tape (see page 14).

Poke a hole with a needle into each bent end of the straw so that a skewer can be inserted to hold the ends together.

Put a dab of hot glue in both holes and insert the bamboo skewer. Repeat for the other straw.

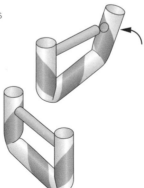

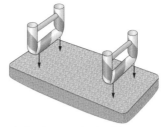

Attach the legs to the bed by running a line of hot glue along the top middle section of the straw. Stick to either end of the bed.

Measure the distance between the leg frames and cut a length of straw to match.

Stick the straw between the two leg frames and against the underside of the bed.

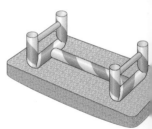

for the bench frame

Cut two 6cm pieces of straw and two 2cm pieces of bamboo skewer for the bench and then follow the bed frame instructions above.

setting
the scene

When I was little, my dinner plate was a source of entertainment rather than sustenance. A meal which included broccoli and mashed potato was bound to become a snowy, tree-clad mountain upon which my fork could slalom down. And if peas were involved, watch out! When making a scene, it is details like mountains and trees, grass and plants that bring play to life and give sense to a world made in miniature. The best thing with these patterns is that we can make our world a fanciful one. Growing up in Australia, I had always heard of a mythical place called 'The Blue Mountains'. In my mind they were a sparkling azure and shrouded with mist. When I grew up, much to my horror, I discovered that this wasn't the case at all. So the mountains I have made are blue, turquoise and pink.

Patterns in this Section

Pine tree
Oak tree
Shrubbery
Mountains
Play mat

pine tree

for the pine tree

dark green DK yarn
brown DK yarn
3.5mm crochet hook
stuffing

yarn suggestion:
I used wool for the trees
because deep down, I am
a tree hugger and there is
nothing better to snuggle
with than wool.

Round 1. Using dark green yarn and a 3.5mm crochet hook, ch2, 6dc into the 2nd ch from hook, ss back into the first dc.

Round 2. *1dc, 2dc into the next st. Repeat from * until the end of the round. (9)

Round 3. *2dc, 2dc into the next st. Repeat from * until the end of the round. (12)

Round 4. *3dc, 2dc into the next st. Repeat from * until the end of the round. (15)

Round 5. *4dc, 2dc into the next st. Repeat from * until the end of the round. (18)

Round 6. 1dc into every st.

Round 7. Working into BLO, *2dc, sk one st. Repeat from * until the end of the round. (12)

Round 8. Working into FLO, *1dc, 2dc into the next st. Repeat from * until the end of the round. (18)

Round 9. *5dc, 2dc into the next st. Repeat from * until the end of the round. (21)

Round 10. *6dc, 2dc into the next st. Repeat from * until the end of the round. (24)

Round 11. *7dc, 2dc into the next st. Repeat from * until the end of the round. (27)

Round 12. *8dc, 2dc into the next st. Repeat from * until the end of the round. (30)

Round 13. 1dc into every st.

Round 14. Working into BLO, *2dc, sk one st. Repeat from* until the end of the round. (20)

Round 15. Working into FLO, *1dc, 2dc into the next st. Repeat from * until the end of the round. (30)

Round 16. *9dc, 2dc into the next st. Repeat from * until the end of the round. (33)

Round 17. *10dc, 2dc into the next st. Repeat from * until the end of the round. (36)

Round 18. *11dc, 2dc into the next st. Repeat from * until the end of the round. (39)

Round 19. *12dc, 2dc into the next st. Repeat from * until the end of the round. (42)

Round 20. *13dc, 2dc into the next st. Repeat from * until the end of the round. (45)

Round 21. 1dc into every st.

Round 22. Working into BLO, *4dc, sk one st. Repeat from * until the end of the round. (36)

Round 23. *3dc, sk one st. Repeat from * until the end of the round. (27)

Round 24. *2dc, sk one st. Repeat from* until the end of the round. (18)

Stuff the tree firmly before continuing.

Round 25. *2dc, sk one st. Repeat from* until the end of the round. (12)

Round 26. Working into BLO, *1dc, sk one st. Repeat from* until the end of the round. (6)

Round 27. Using brown yarn and working into the unused loops of Round 25, 12dc, ss back into the first dc. (12)

Round 28. 1dc into every st.

Round 29. *1dc, 2dc into the next st. Repeat from * until the end of the round. (18)

Fasten off.

oak tree

for the oak tree

green DK yarn
brown flecked DK yarn
3.5mm crochet hook
stuffing

yarn suggestion:
As for the Pine Tree.

Round 1. Using green yarn and a 3.5mm crochet hook, ch2. Work 6dc into the 2nd ch from hook, ss back into the first dc.
Round 2. 2dc into every st. (12)
Round 3. *1dc, 2dc into the next st. Repeat from * until the end of the round. (18)
Round 4. *5dc, 2dc into the next st. Repeat from * until the end of the round. (21)
Round 5. *6dc, 2dc into the next st. Repeat from * until the end of the round. (24)
Round 6. *7dc, 2dc into the next st. Repeat from * until the end of the round. (27)
Round 7. *8dc, 2dc into the next st. Repeat from * until the end of the round. (30)
Round 8. *9dc, 2dc into the next st. Repeat from * until the end of the round. (33)
Round 9. *10dc, 2dc into the next st. Repeat from * until the end of the round. (36)
Round 10. *11dc, 2dc into the next st. Repeat from * until the end of the round. (39)
Round 11. *12dc, 2dc into the next st. Repeat from * until the end of the round. (42)
Round 12. *13dc, 2dc into the next st. Repeat from * until the end of the round. (45)
Rounds 13–19. 1dc into every st.
Round 20. *4dc, sk one st. Repeat from * until the end of the round. (36)
Round 21. *5dc, sk one st. Repeat from * until the end of the round. (30)
Round 22. *4dc, sk one st. Repeat from * until the end of the round. (24)

Round 23. *3dc, sk one st. Repeat from * until the end of the round. (18)
Stuff.
Round 24. *2dc, sk one st. Repeat from * until the end of the round. (12)
Round 25. Working into BLO, *1dc, sk one st. Repeat from* until the end of the round. (6)
Fasten off.
Round 26. Using brown yarn and and working into the unused loops of Round 25, 12 dc, ss back into the first dc. (12)
Round 27. 1dc into every st. (12)
Round 28. *1dc, 2dc into the next st. Repeat from* until the end of the round. (18)
Fasten off.

for the pointy topped oak

Round 1. Using green yarn and a 3.5mm crochet hook, ch2, 6dc into the 2nd ch from hook, ss back into the first dc.
Round 2. *1dc , 2dc into the next st. Repeat from * until the end of the round. (9)
Round 3. *2dc, 2dc into the next st. Repeat from * until the end of the round. (12)
Round 4. *3dc, 2dc into the next st. Repeat from * until the end of the round. (15)
Round 5. *4dc, 2dc into the next st. Repeat from * until the end of the round. (18)
Rounds 6–30. As Rounds 4–28 for the Oak tree.

shrubbery

Foundation row. Using green yarn and a 4mm crochet hook, ch100.

Row 1. *Starting in 2nd ch from hook, 3dc, ch4. Repeat from * one more time, ss back into the foundation ch. *Ch4, starting in 2nd ch from hook, 3dc, ch4, ss back into the foundation ch. Repeat from * until the end of the foundation ch.

Scrunch up the crocheted chain and sew into a shrubby shape.

mountains

for the mountain

2 x 50g balls
of cream DK yarn

2 x 50g balls of pink,
navy blue or turquoise DK yarn

5.5mm crochet hook

stuffing

needle

yarn suggestion: As with the trees, I have used wool for the mountains because I can quite imagine snuggling up on the couch with one of these.

Note: Two balls of yarn are worked together so that it is similar to a chunky ply. While three colours are recommended for the mountain, the instructions in this pattern will refer to a pink version.

for the insets

The insets are crocheted half circles that are added into a round in order to give the mountain its jagged look. An inset is attached in the following way:
Place the flat side of the inset along four crocheted stitches in the round as indicated by the pattern. Sew the flat base of the inset to the four stitches and then crochet around the 6dc of the inset as directed.

Make 6 insets using a 5.5mm crochet hook, three in cream yarn (C) and 3 in the main colour (which for this mountain will be pink (P)).

Row 1. Holding two strands of yarn together and using a 5.5mm crochet hook, ch2, 3dc into the second ch from the hook. Ch1, turn. (3)

Row 2. 2dc into each st. (6)
Fasten off, leaving a 30cm tail.

for the mountain

Round 1. Using two strands of cream yarn and a 5.5mm crochet hook, ch2, 4dc into the second ch from hook, ss back into the first dc. (4)

Round 2. *1dc, 2dc into the next st. Repeat from * one more time. (6)

Round 3. *2dc, 2dc into the next st. Repeat from * one more time. (8)

Round 4. *3dc, 2dc into the next st. Repeat from * one more time. (10)

Round 5. *4dc, 2dc into the next st. Repeat from * one more time. (12)

Round 6. Sew a cream inset to the first four sts. Into the inset, (1dc into each st) 8dc into the rest of the round. (14)

Round 7. *2dc, 2dc into the next st. Repeat from * one more time, 8dc. (16)

Round 8. *3dc, 2dc into the next st. Repeat from * one more time, 8dc. (18)

Round 9. 1dc into every st.

Round 10. 13dc, sew a cream inset to the next 4sts. Into the inset, (*1dc, 2dc into the next st. Repeat from* two more times). 1dc. (23)

Rounds 11–12. 1dc into every st.
Both cream (C) and pink (P) yarns will be used from this point. Carry unused colour behind work.

Round 13. In C, *3dc, 2dc into the next st. Repeat from * two more times. 6dc. In P, 4dc. In C, 1dc. (26)

Round 14. In C, 4dc, sew a cream inset to the next 4sts. Into the inset, (*1dc, 2dc into the next st. Repeat from * two more times). 12dc. In P, 6dc. (31)

Round 15. In C, 15dc. In P, 2dc. Using cream, 7dc. Using pink, 7dc.

Round 16. In C, 14dc. In P, 4dc. In C, 5dc. In P, 8dc.

Round 17. In P, 2dc. In C, 11dc. In P, 6dc. In C, 3dc. In P, 9dc.

Round 18. In P, 3dc. In C, 9dc. In P, 2dc, sew a pink inset to the next 4sts. Into the inset, (*1dc then 2dc into the next st. Repeat from * two more times). 2dc. In C, 2dc. In P, 9dc. (36).

Round 19. In P, 4dc. In C, 7dc. In P, 17dc, 2dc into the next st. *1dc then 2dc into the next st. Repeat from * one more time. 3dc. (39)

Round 20. In P, 5dc. In C, 5dc. In P, 29dc.

Round 21. Sew a pink inset to the next 4sts. In P, into the inset, (*1dc, 2dc into the next st. Repeat from * twice more). 2dc. In C, 3dc. In P, 30dc. (44)
Continue using pink yarn only.

Rounds 22–23. 1dc into every st.

Round 24. 28dc, sew an inset to the next 4sts. Into the inset, (*2dc then 2dc into the next st. Repeat from * one more time). 12dc. (48)

Rounds 25–29. 1dc into every st.

Round 30. *11dc, 2dc into the next st. Repeat from * until the end of the round. (52)

Round 31. 1dc into every st.

Round 32. *12dc, 2dc into the next st. Repeat from * until the end of the round. (56)

Rounds 33–36. 1dc into every st.

Round 37. *6dc, sk one next st. Repeat from* until the end of the round. (48)
Stuff the peak.

Round 38. *7dc, sk one st. Repeat from* until the end of the round. (42)

Round 39. *6dc , sk one st. Repeat from* until the end of the round. (36)

Round 40. *5dc, sk one st. Repeat from* until the end of the round. (30)

Round 41. *4dc, sk one st. Repeat from* until the end of the round. (24)

Round 42. *3dc, sk one st. Repeat from* until the end of the round. (18)
Stuff the body firmly.

Round 43. *2dc, sk one st. Repeat from* until the end of the round. (12)

Round 44. *1dc, sk one st. Repeat from* until the end of the round. (6)
Fasten off.

play mat

for the play mat

9 x 50g balls of 12ply green yarn
pale pink 4ply yarn
yellow 4ply yarn
pale pink 4ply yarn
4.5mm crochet hook
2.5mm crochet hook

yarn suggestion:
Soft wool that a little chin might
like to rest upon.

special stitch: dtr bobble

*With the hook facing down, wrap the yarn twice around the crochet hook then insert the hook through the stitch/chain. Grab the yarn then pull it back through the stitch/chain. Grab the yarn again and draw it through the first two loops. Grab the yarn again and pull it through the next two loops. Repeat into the same st/ch from * three more times. There should now be five loops on the hook. Grab the yarn and pull it through all five loops.

for the mat

Foundation row. Using green yarn and a 4.5mm hook, ch102.
Row 1. Starting in 3rd ch from hook, 100htr. Ch2, turn. (100)
Rows 2–64. 1htr into every st. Ch2, turn.
Round 65. 100dc along the top, 96dc down the side (1dc into the first row end, 2dc into the next row end), 100dc along the bottom, 96dc up the other side (1dc into the first row end, 2dc into the next row end), ss back into the first dc. (392)
Round 66. *Ch4, sk the next 3 sts, ss into the following st. Repeat from* until the end of the round.
Round 67. (2dc, ch3, 2dc) into every 4chsp around. (392)
Round 68. (1dc, 1tr, 1dtr bobble, ch1, 1tr, 1dc) into every 3chsp around. (490)
Round 69. (1dc then ch4, 1dc into the next 1chsp) into every 1chsp around.
Round 70. (2dc, ch3, 2dc) into every 4chsp around. Fasten off.

for the flowers

Round 1. Using any 4ply yarn and a 2.5mm hook, ch4, ss back into the first st.
Round 2. Into the ch4 loop, 10dc, ss back into the first dc.
Round 3. *5dc into the first st, ss into the next st. Repeat from * until the end of the round.

Fasten off then sew to the mat.
Repeat in different colours to create a wildflower meadow.

dressing *up*

Embrace your whimsy and invite all of your old toys to bring these scenes to life. I love the thought of a menagerie of creatures spending the night together in the lake cabin, a goose stumbling upon a caravan or a dog rugged up with a scarf in a sailboat. While the measurements are directed towards Playmobil proportions, you should find that they fit a variety of small toys.

Patterns in this Section

Scarf
Beanie
Backpack
Ice cream seller
Cape
Tutu

for the scarf

Turquoise 4ply yarn

2.5mm crochet hook

for the beanie

pale lilac 4ply yarn

cream 4ply yarn

2.5mm crochet hook

for the backpack

tan 4ply yarn

2.5mm crochet hook

medium-size bead
or small button

cotton sewing thread
and needle

for the scarf

Foundation row. Using a 2.5mm crochet hook, ch30.

Row 1. Starting in 2nd ch from hook, 29dc. Fasten off.

for the beanie

Foundation round. Using pale lilac yarn and a 2.5mm crochet hook, ch19, ss back into the first ch.

Rounds 1–4. 1dc into every st. (18)

Round 5. *2dc, sk one st. Repeat from * until the end of the round. (12)

Round 6. *1dc, sk one st. Repeat from * until the end of the round. Fasten off. (6)

for the bobble

Round 1. Using cream yarn, ch2, 6dc into the 2nd ch from hook, ss back into the first dc. Fasten off. (6)

Sew the edges together to form a little bobble and sew to the top of the beanie.

Fold the brim of the beanie up.

for the backpack

Foundation row. Beginning at the bottom of the backpack, using tan yarn and a 2.5mm crochet hook, ch7.

Row 1. Starting in 2nd ch from hook, 6dc. Ch1, turn. (6)

Row 2. 1dc into every st. Ch1, turn.

Round 3. 1dc into every st around each side. (14)

Rounds 4–9. 1dc into every st side.

Row 10. Ch1, turn, 6dc. Ch1, turn. (6)

Row 11. 1dc into every st. Ch1, turn.

Row 12. 3dc, ch4, 3dc.

Fasten off, leaving a 40cm tail. Thread the tail with a needle then weave the needle through to the back at the side edge of Round 9.

Make a loop with the tail from the top of the backpack to the bottom to form a shoulder strap. Measure against your toy to ensure it fits, then fasten off. Repeat with the other side.

Sew a button or bead to the front of the backpack.

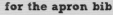

ice cream seller

for the ice cream seller's outfit

cream 4ply yarn
pale blue 4ply yarn
2.5mm crochet hook

for the hat
Foundation round. Using cream yarn and 2.5mm crochet hook, ch7.
Round 1. Starting in 2nd ch from hook, 5dc, 2dc into the last ch, 5dc along the opposite side of the foundation ch. (12)
Round 2. 5dc, 2dc into each of the next 2sts, 5dc. (14)
Round 3. 6dc, 2dc into each of the next 2sts, 6dc. (16)
Round 4. 7dc, 2dc into each of the next 2sts, 7dc. (18)
Round 5. Change to pale blue yarn, 1dc into every st. Fasten off.

for the apron bib
Foundation row. Using cream yarn and a 2.5mm crochet hook, ch6.
Row 1. Starting in 2nd ch from hook, 5dc. Ch1, turn. (5)
Rows 2–3. 1dc into every st. Ch 1, turn.
Row 4. 1dc into every st. Fasten off.

for the apron skirt
Foundation row. Using cream yarn, ch9.
Row 1. Starting in 2nd ch from hook, 8dc. Ch1, turn. (8)
Row 2. 1dc into every st. Ch 1, turn.
Row 3. 1dc into every st. Fasten off.
Using the pale blue yarn, leave a long tail on either side and work 8dc along the top of Row 1.

Sew the bib to the skirt and use the tails to tie the apron on with.

Attach a loop of pale blue yarn to the two top edges of the bib to form the neck strap.

for the cape

pale blue 4ply yarn
cream 4ply yarn
yellow 4ply yarn
2.5mm crochet hook

for the tutu

tulle, approx. 26 x 5cm
cotton sewing thread and needle
sparkly yarn
glue

for the cape

Foundation row. Using pale blue yarn and a 2.5mm crochet hook, ch8.

Row 1. Starting in 2nd ch from hook, 7dc. (7)

Rows 2–7. 1dc into every st. Ch1, turn.

Row 8. 1dc into every st. Fasten off.

Round 9. Using cream yarn, work 1dc into each st, (1dc, ch2, 1dc) into each corner st. (32)

Row 10. Using yellow yarn, leave a long tail on either side, 1dc into every st across the top of the cape.

Use the tails to tie the cape.

for the tutu

Cut 2 pieces of tulle, approximately 13 x 2.5cm. Fold in half lengthways then sew a gathering stitch just under the folded line.

Pull tight until the tutu can wrap around the figurine's waist and sew the back together.

Using the sparkly yarn, wrap around the top of the tutu to hide the stitching and secure at the back with a small dab of glue.

index

2 treble crochet cluster stitch 39
3 treble cluster stitch 39
3 triple crochet together stitch 84

abbreviations 13
appliqué ice creams 52
apron 108

backpack 107
bamboo skewers 14, 17
banks (lake) 79
beanie hat 107
beds 37, 71, 96
beginning work 8–9
benches 37, 96
blackboards 54
blankets 39–40, 71, 93
boats 73–5, 82–91
bobbles 107
bunk beds 37
bunting 14, 17, 28
button loops 35, 49

cabins
  boat 89–91
  log/wood 60–5
campfire 27
Canal Boat Idyll 82–97
canoe 76–7
cape 109
Caravan Wishes 30–43
caravans 32–6
Carefree Camping 18–29
chain stitch 10
chimney 72
colour changes 13
construction materials 17
crochet hooks 8–9, 17
crochet techniques 8–16
cupboards 41–3
cups 43
cushions 38

daisy stitch 16
doors 35, 43, 65, 72, 90
double crochet stitch 11
double treble bobble stitch 105

double treble crochet stitch 12
drawers 42
Dressing Up 106–9

embroidery 25
  stitches 15–16

fastening off 13
faucets 42
finishing techniques 14–16
flowers 105
freezer, chest 56
French knots 15
frying pan 28

gables 64–5
glue 17
greenery 68, 69, 78, 95, 100–2
grill, van 49, 51

half treble crochet stitch 11
hats 107, 108
headlights 51
hubcaps 36, 51
hydrangea 68

ice cream seller outfit 108–9
Ice Cream Supreme 44–57
ice cream van 46–9
ice creams 52–3, 55
ice lollies 52–3, 55
islands 80

jetty 67

kitchen sink 41, 42

lake mat 78–80
Lakeside Supreme 58–81
lawns 78
life preserver 92

materials 16–17
mountains 103–4

oak trees 101

paddles 77
patterns, reading 13
picnic basket 26
picnic rug 26

pillows 38
pin-striped patterns 35
pine trees 100
play mat 105
pot plants 68, 95
projects
    Canal Boat Idyll 82–97
    Caravan Wishes 30–43
    Carefree Camping 18–29
    Dressing Up 106–9
    Ice Cream Supreme 44–57
    Lakeside Supreme 58–81
    Setting the Scene 98–105

roofs 47–8, 62–4, 90
room dividers 94
rounds, working 12
rows, working 12
rugs 23, 26, 71

sailboat 73–5
scarf 107
Setting the Scene 98–105
shrubbery 102
sleeping bag 22

sleeping mat 22
slip knots 9
slipstitch 10

taps 42
teepee rug 23
teepee 24–5
tents 20–1
treble crochet stitch 12
trees 100–1
tutu 109
tyres 36, 51

van, ice cream 46–51

wadding (batting) 17
washi tape bunting 14, 17
water 78
wheels 36, 51
window box 69
window shutters 49
windows 36, 49–50, 65, 90–1
windscreen 49, 50
wood burner 72, 95

yarns 16

acknowledgements

There is no way that any of this project could have been achieved without the help of my husband Jonno. He would roll out of bed at crazy hours in the morning, milk the cows, ferry boys about, listen patiently to all of my 'requests' and still have enough kindness to last throughout the day. I don't know how you do it but I am so lucky that you are mine. Thank you.

Archie and Hugo, your excitement for all of the projects brought them to life. I will never forget the disaster scene on the lake I found one morning! Thank you.

Tim and Lucy at The Old Forge in Dorset who let us stay in their two beautiful Shepherd's Huts, spoilt us rotten and let us explore their vintage caravan and gypsy wagon. So much inspiration for this book came from your place. Now I have my own caravan too! Thank you.

Sophie, I can't believe that I get to have you as my editor! Your calm responses to my chaotic emails, your cheer and gold stars have made this process a joy. Thank you.

Keiko and Christine, who turned this book into such a beautiful world that I now have to develop a shrink ray so I can live there. And to Kang for the illustrations. Thank you.

Katie, for ironing the manuscript so beautifully. Thank you.

Joanne, holy mac the stars were in alignment the day you agreed to become my tech editor. These patterns are glossy because of you! Thank you.

Kyle and Judith, for letting me make this book with you; it has been a dream. Thank you.

Playmobil, for allowing us to use their figures. (With kind permission of Geobra Brandstätter GmbH & Co. KG, Germany. PLAYMOBIL is a registered trademark of Geobra Brandstätter GmbH & Co. KG, for which also the displayed PLAYMOBIL toy figures are protected.) Thank you.

Mum, for your shining example of how to be and for always keeping me well stocked with crafty supplies, encouragement and love. Thank you.

Shirley and Lou, for teaching me how to embroider. That was the start of everything! Thank you.

Norm and Maureen, I promise the next time I ring, it won't be to ask for favour #9133448. You are the best in-laws in the world! Thank you.

And to my family and friends who I have mercilessly neglected during this process and yet still love me. Thank you.